Boho Crochet

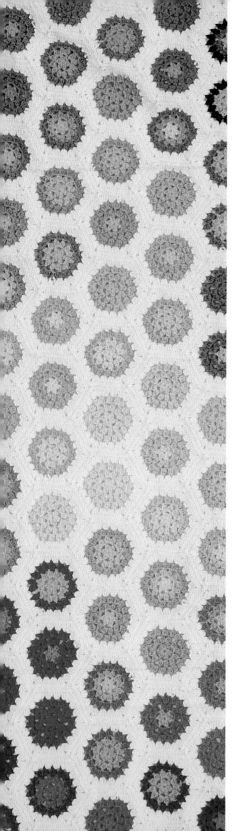

A Quantum Book

First published in the USA in 2015 by

Martingale®
19021 120th Ave. NE, Ste. 102
Bothell, WA 98011-9511 USA
ShopMartingale.com

Library of Congress Cataloging-in-Publication Data is available upon request.

ISBN: 978-1-60468-551-0

Mission Statement
Dedicated to providing quality products and service to inspire creativity.

This book was conceived, designed, and produced by
Quantum Books Ltd.
6 Blundell Street
London N7 9BH
United Kingdom

Publisher: Kerry Enzor
Project Editor: Hazel Eriksson
Editor: Julie Brooke
Designer: Blanche Williams of Harper Williams Design
Photographer: Simon Pask
Technical Consultants: Carol Meldrum and Sophie Scott
Production Manager: Rohana Yusof

Printed in China by 1010 Printing International Ltd.

20 19 18 17 16   8 7 6 5 4 3 2

Boho Crochet

30 Hip and Happy Projects

Martingale®
Create with Confidence

CONTENTS

Introduction

I've always loved the bohemian style of the late 1960s and early 1970s and I cannot resist the amazing patterns and colors that were used on everything from clothing to carpets and posters to wallpaper. Crochet was an integral part of the look then, and I have been delighted to watch it come back into fashion and give me the chance to explore it myself.

For me, the bohemian style represents creativity in its purest form: the combination of amazing colors, often inspired by nature; textures and fabrics that feel amazing to the touch; and exciting stitch patterns that will rock your world.

The original bohemian, free-spirited people who founded the look and gave it a name, were thought to be unconventional. If you, like me, are one of today's boho followers, then embrace this freedom and explore the style on your own terms by giving the patterns in this book your own twist—add tassels, use your own color palette, or use thicker or thinner hooks and yarns to maximize or minimize the designs. Make every project unique to you.

I am really proud to present this amazing collection of crochet projects. You'll find quick-and-easy makes like pillows and coasters, as well as larger, more time-consuming items such as scarves and blankets. They come from a very talented group of bloggers and crafters (see pages 8–9) who will show you a fantastic range of crochet techniques, and will inject a rainbow-colored wave of bohemian chic into your home and wardrobe.

Go wild with boho color and see how it can inspire you on a daily basis!

Winh

The DESIGNERS

Amy Astle

Color, crochet, and anything crafty make Amy Astle of Little Doolally happy. She has been crocheting since she was ten years old: Her grandma bought her some old 1970s weekly sewing, knitting, and crochet magazines from a yard sale and she has been hooked ever since. She discovered her love for yarn, surface pattern, and texture while studying for a degree in textiles. Since then, her fingers have been itching to delve into the wonderful world of crochet and inspire and teach other like-minded people at www.littledoolally.com. She lives in Nottinghamshire, UK.

Annemarie Benthem

Annemarie lives in Delft in the Netherlands. She took her first crochet class in 2010 and immediately fell in love with it. There aren't many projects she hasn't tried, and although she loves to make other people's patterns, she also loves to design herself. She hopes to inspire people with her designs. You can find more designs on her blog, www.annemarieshaakblog .blogspot.com, and her Etsy shop, www.etsy.com/shop /annemariesbreiblog.

Ruth Bramham

Ruth, known online as Ruthie Joy, taught herself to knit and crochet to make clothes for her son Paul when he was a baby. She lives in Lancashire, UK, along with her husband Adrian and an enormous yarn and bead stash! Taking inspiration from nature she enjoys making accessories from natural yarns such as wool, mohair, and silk. She also creates jewelry from semi-precious stones, freshwater pearls, and Czech glass. When not making things she loves to walk in her beloved Yorkshire Dales and Lake District. Her work can be found at www.etsy .com/uk/shop/Yarnhappiness.

Ali Campbell

Ali remembers getting hooked on crochet as a child. Today, she always has two or three projects on the go and teaches it to others. She says: "With just one little hook and a small ball of wool this eco-friendly craft will keep you occupied like you never thought it could!" She lives in Dorset, UK. Find her online at www.gethookedoncrochet.co.uk.

Susan Carlson

Susan describes herself as a cheerful, creative, crochet designer, and collector of all things colorful. She was taught to crochet as a young girl by her granny and her first project was a long scarf for her dad. Although crochet and other craftiness have always been part of her life, she channeled her energy into teaching junior high and high school sciences for many years before she picked up a hook again and her blog, Felted Button, was born. Susan loves all things colorful—especially with buttons and yarn! Her designs can be found at FeltedButton .com. She lives in Utah.

Sara Dudek

Sara started crocheting when she was 12 years old and began designing patterns soon after. She started Sans Limites Crochet (sanslimitescrochet .blogspot.co.uk) after college and has loved watching it grow. Her crochet work has taken her to craft fairs around the United States and even included designs for the non-profit company Krochet Kids International. She has an Etsy store and currently lives in Colorado where she spends her days studying design in graduate school, teaching dance, and exploring the Rocky Mountains.

Carmen Heffernan

Carmen lives in the Irish countryside with her husband and their delightful dogs and cats. Her mother and aunts were all creative and skillful at needlework, so it has always been a part of her life. Carmen is passionate about crochet and color and feels driven to create every day! She also loves to teach crochet, and to inspire others to express themselves with hooks and yarn. Carmen especially loves taking simple patterns and using different or surprising color combinations to create something vibrant and beautiful. She documents her crochet creations on Instagram, at http://instagram.com /anniedesigncrochet, and sells her colorful crochet flowers on Etsy (www.etsy.com/shop /AnnieDesign).

Dorien Hollewijn

Ever since she was a little girl Dorien has been playing with yarn and fabric. Her doll had a huge wardrobe of knitted, crocheted, and sewn garments. A few years ago, when circumstances kept her at home, she immediately picked up yarn and fabrics to keep her occupied. And because she learned so much about all crafts from other bloggers she started her own blog (madebydo.blogspot.nl) about her adventures in the world of fiber. Her work emphasizes the possibilities of color: she says that creating a simple square or hexagon over and again with different colors, and then arranging them into one gorgeous blanket, is the best game ever. She has an Etsy store, (www.etsy .com/uk/shop/JustDo), and lives in the Netherlands.

Sandra Paul

Sandra Paul is a craft blogger and pattern designer who loves to crochet, knit, and sew. She lives in a small village in Bedfordshire, UK, with her husband, daughter and an ever-expanding stash of yarn and fabric. Re-discovering knitting as an adult by dusting off some rusty childhood skills one Christmas day, it was only a matter of weeks before she knew that she needed to learn crochet too. One how-to book and a stressful evening of fumbled fingers later, a slightly crooked granny square and a brand new obsession had been born. Her designs can be found at www.cherryheart.co.uk.

Marinke Slump

Marinke (known online as Wink) is a blogger and designer, who came to the attention of the crochet community for her colorful mandalas. She first learned to crochet from a small book on how to make amigurumi. Armed with some cotton yarn and a crochet hook that was way too small, she taught herself the single crochet stitch. Her first crochet project was supposed to become a fish, but turned out as a little pig... Now, five years later, the art of crochet feels second nature to her, and she even has her dream job of being a full-time crochet blogger! Wink writes patterns on a regular basis for online and offline magazines including *Tuts+* and *Simply Crochet*, and shares patterns on her blog (acreativebeing.com) and her Etsy and Ravelry shops. She lives and works from her home in the Netherlands. Find her online at acreativebeing.com.

Project SELECTOR

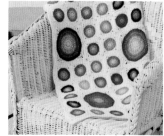

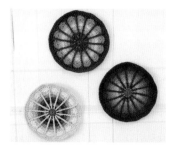

Crochet for the
HOME

Cozy throws and pillows bring boho charm
to your home. Use one or two pieces to bring
a splash of color to a sofa or easy chair—or
transform a room into a kaleidoscope of
crocheted accessories.

Vintage Fan Ripple Blanket

This pretty pattern was inspired by a vintage design, and the simple pattern repeat means it can be easily adapted to make a smaller baby blanket or larger throw.

YOU WILL NEED

DK-weight cotton/acrylic blend yarn (approx 1.76 oz/50 g; 153 yds/140 m)

CCa   2 balls in olive
CCb   2 balls in pink
CCc   2 balls in pale pink
CCd   2 balls in red
CCe   2 balls in violet
CCf   2 balls in yellow
CCg   2 balls in blue

Size G-6 (4mm) hook

Gauge
Gauge is not important in this project

Dimensions
Approx 56" x 56"

To make the blanket

All stitches are worked into the back loops only throughout. To make a larger or smaller blanket, start with a chain which is a multiple of 9 plus 1. Using CCa, ch280

Row 1: sc1 into 2nd ch from hook, sc1 into next ch3, *sc3 into next ch, sc1 into next ch8, rep from *, ending last rep after four of the sc8 have been worked, turn. (330sts)

Rows 2–3: ch1, *skip 1st, sc1 into next 4sts, sc3 into next st, sc1 into next 4sts, skip 1st, rep from * to end.

Row 4: sl st into first 3sts, ch6 (counts as trtr1), trtr1 into next 2sts, trtr3 into next st, trtr1 into next 3sts, skip next 2sts, *skip next 2sts, trtr1 into next 3sts, trtr3 into next st, trtr1 into next 3sts, skip next 2sts, rep from * to end, turn.

Fasten off yarn and join in CCb.

Row 5: ch1, *sc1 into next 4sts, sc3 into next st, sc1 into next 4sts, rep from * to end.

Rows 2–5 form pattern repeat. Repeat these rows, changing color after Row 4 on each repeat as follows.

Rows 6–8: CCb.
Rows 9–12: CCc.
Rows 13–16: CCd.
Rows 17–20: CCe.
Rows 21–24: CCf.
Rows 25–28: CCg.

Repeat stripe sequence until blanket is the required size. On the last repeat do not fasten off yarn after Row 4 but repeat Rows 5, 2, and 3 to form the edge.

Finishing

Fasten off yarn and weave in loose ends. Block if required.

Annie Blanket

SKILL LEVEL

Dotted stripes add a playful touch of color to this baby blanket. You can use a different
color for each stripe, or restrict yourself to one or two.

YOU WILL NEED

DK-weight cotton yarn (approx 1.76 oz/50 g;
109 yds/100 m)
MC   5 balls in white
CC   Scraps of yarn in 12 colors
Size E-4 (3.5mm) hook

Gauge
18 stitches by 9 rows over 4" square using
dc; however gauge is not essential for this
pattern

Dimensions
Approx 21" x 24"

To make the blanket
To make a larger/smaller blanket,
work your chain in a number
divisible by 3, plus 2.
Using MC, ch101.
Row 1: sc1 into 2nd ch from hook,
sc1 into each ch to end, turn.
(100sts)
Row 2: ch2 (counts as first dc), dc2
into first st, *skip 2sts, dc3 into next
st, rep from * to end, turn. (34 sets
of dc3)
Fasten off MC and join in CC of
choice.
Row 3: ch3 (counts as sc1 and ch2),
*sc1 in between next two groups of
dc3, ch2, rep from *, ending last rep
with sc1 into top of ch2 at beg of
previous row.
Fasten off CC and join in MC.
Row 4: ch2 (counts as first dc), dc2
into first ch2sp, *skip next st, dc3
into next ch2sp, rep from * to end.
Fasten off MC and join in CC.
Rows 3–4 form pattern. Repeat until

74 rows of pattern have been worked
or until blanket is required length.
Do not fasten off yarn.
Row 75: ch1, sc1 into each st
to end.
Fasten off yarn and weave in
loose ends.

Edging
Using MC, join yarn to any sc on
last row worked.
Round 1: ch1, sc1 into same st as
you joined yarn to, sc1 into each st
to corner, sc3 into corner st (first
corner made), work sc1 into each
st down the side of the blanket to
corner, sc3 into corner st (second
corner made), sc1 into each st along
edge to next corner, sc3 into corner
st (third corner made), sc1 into
each st up the side of the blanket
to corner, sc3 into corner st (fourth
corner made), sc1 to end, sl st into
ch1 at beg of round.

Round 2: ch1, sc1 into first st, *sc1 into each st to center st of sc3 corner, sc3 into corner st, rep from * until all corners have been worked, sc1 into each st to end, sl st into ch1 at beg of round.

Round 3: as Round 2.
Fasten off yarn and weave in loose ends.

Finishing
Block if required.

Daisy Baby Blanket

SKILL LEVEL

Colorful daisies are scattered over this pretty blanket. This size is perfect for a baby's crib, but why not make a larger one for picnics?

YOU WILL NEED

Sport-weight cotton yarn (approx 3.5 oz/ 100 g; 299 yds/273 m)

MC	2 balls in cream
CCa	1 ball in orange
CCb	1 ball in light orange
CCc	1 ball in yellow
CCd	1 ball in light pink
CCe	1 ball in dark pink
CCf	1 ball in purple
CCg	1 ball in beige
CCh	1 ball in green

Size F-5 (3.75mm) hook

Gauge
Gauge is not important in this project

Dimensions
Approx 30" x 36"

Special stitches

dc3cluster: work as dc3tog working each dc into the same st or space to make a cluster.

dc4cluster: work as dc4tog working each dc into the same st or space to make a cluster.

To make the blanket

DAISY WHEEL SQUARE (MAKE 30)

Using CC of choice, ch5, join ends with sl st to form ring.

Round 1: ch1 (counts as first st), sc11 into ring, sl st into ch1 at beg of round. (12sts)

Round 2: ch4 (count as dc1 and ch1), *dc1 into next st, ch1, rep from * to end, sl st into third of ch4 at beg of round. (12 ch1sp)
Fasten off yarn.
Join in MC into any of the ch1sp from previous round.

Round 3: ch3 (counts as first st), dc3cluster into same ch1sp, ch3, *dc4cluster into next ch1sp, ch3, rep from * to end, sl st into top of first cluster. (12 clusters)
Fasten off MC and join in next CC of choice into any of the ch3sp from previous round.

Round 4: ch4 (counts as first st), work [tr2, ch3, tr3] into same ch3sp (corner made), dc3 into next two ch3sp, *work [tr3, ch3, tr3] into next ch3sp (corner made), dc3 into next two ch3sp, rep from * to end, sl st into top of ch4 at beg of round. (4 ch3sp)

Round 5: sl st across sts and into first ch3sp, ch3 (counts as first st), work [dc2, ch3, dc3] into same ch3sp (corner made), [skip next 3sts, dc3 in between next 2sts] 3 times, *work [dc3, ch3, dc3] into next ch3sp (corner made), [skip next 3sts, dc3 in between next 2sts] 3 times, rep from * to end, sl st into top of ch3 at beg of round. (20 sets of dc3)
Fasten off CC and join in MC to any of the stitches on previous round.

Round 6: ch3 (counts as first st), *dc1 into each st until ch3sp, work [dc2, ch3, dc2] into ch3sp, rep from * 3 times more, dc1 into each st to end of round, sl st into top of ch3 at beg of round. (76sts)

Round 7: ch1 (counts as first st), *sc1 into each st until ch3sp, work [sc1, ch1, sc1] into ch3sp, rep from * 3 times more, sc1 into each st to end of round, sl st into ch1 at beg of round.

Fasten off yarn and weave in loose ends.

Finishing

Lay out squares in your choice of design in six rows made up of five squares across. Using MC, hold first two squares with wrong sides together and sl st into corner space of both squares.

Ch1, sc1 into same place, work sc1 into matching sts from both squares up to next corner, sc1 into corner.

Do not break off yarn but join next two squares together as given above until five sets of two squares have been joined.

Join the next row of squares to the first row of squares. Continue joining as set until all squares have been joined.

Next join the squares vertically as given for the rows, sl st over sections where the squares are already joined.

Border

Use MC for the first and last round of border, and three CC shades for Rounds 2–4 of border.

Using MC and with RS facing you, join with sl st to any st on outer edge of blanket.

Round 1: ch1, sc1 into each st and chsp until first corner, work [sc1, ch1, sc1] into first corner, *sc1 into each st and chsp to next corner**, work [sc1, ch1, sc1] into corner, rep from *, ending last rep at **.

Fasten off MC and join first CC of choice into any st from previous round.

Round 2: ch2, hdc1 into each st until first corner, work [hdc1, ch1, hdc1] into first corner, *hdc1 into each st and chsp to next corner**, work [hdc1, ch1, hdc1] into corner, rep from *, ending last rep at **.

Fasten off CC and join second CC of choice into any st from previous round.

Round 3: as Round 2.

Fasten off CC and join third CC of choice into any st from previous round.

Round 4: as Round 2.

Fasten of CC and join in MC into any st from previous round.

Round 5: ch1, sc1 into same st, ch2, hdc1 into sc just worked, skip next st, *sc1 into next st, ch2, hdc1 into sc just worked, skip next st, rep from * to end.

Fasten off yarn and weave in loose ends. Block if required.

Join the daisy wheel squares together to create a field of colorful blooms. Arrange the different colors in rows or place them in a random order.

Color Wheel Hexagon Blanket

Pinwheeling hexagons are an interesting spin on classic granny squares. But it's the color placement, based on the color wheel, that makes this blanket so eye-catchingly special.

YOU WILL NEED

Sport-weight cotton yarn (approx 1.76 oz/
50 g; 176 yds/161 m)
MC   16 balls in white
CC   Approx 1 oz/25 g each of 24
       additional assorted colors
Size G-6 (4mm) hook

Gauge
A hexagon measures 3½" wide

Dimensions
58" x 52"

To make the blanket

The blanket is made with white-bordered hexagons with circles that gradually change in color from pale colors in the center, to darker colors around the outsides.

Start the first hexagon using the same CC for the first three rounds and the MC for the last two rounds. For the second hexagon add new CCa for first round, then complete as the first hexagon.

For the third hexagon work first two rounds using CCa and complete as first hexagon.

For the fourth hexagon work first round in CCb, the second round in CCa, and the third round in CC and complete as first hexagon.

HEXAGON MOTIF (MAKE 252)

Using CC of choice, make magic loop.

Round 1: ch3 (counts as first dc), dc2tog into ring, ch3, *dc3tog, ch3, rep from * four more times, sl st into top of ch3 at beg of round. (6 clusters)
Sl st into next ch3sp.

Round 2: ch3 (counts as first dc), work [dc2tog, ch3, dc3tog] into same ch3sp, ch1, *work [dc3tog, ch3, dc3tog] into next ch3sp, ch1, rep from * to end, sl st into top of ch3 at beg of round. (12 clusters)
Sl st into next ch3sp.

Round 3: ch3 (counts as first dc), work [dc2tog, ch3, dc3tog] into same ch3sp, ch1, dc3tog into next ch1sp, *ch1, work [dc3tog, ch3, dc3tog] into next ch3sp, ch1, dc3tog into next ch1sp, ch1, rep from * to end, sl st into top of ch3 at beg of round. (18 clusters)
Fasten off yarn and join in MC.
Sl st into next ch3sp.

Round 4: ch3 (counts as first dc), work [dc2, ch2, dc3] into same ch3sp, work [dc3 into next ch1sp] twice, *work [dc3, ch2, dc3] into next ch3sp, work [dc3 into next ch1sp] twice, rep from * to end, sl st into top of ch3 at beg of round. (24 sets of dc3)

Round 5: ch1 (counts as first sc), work sc1 into each stitch and sc2 into each ch2sp to end, sl st into ch1 at beg of round. (84sts)

Fasten off yarn and weave in loose ends.

Finishing

Using picture as guide, keep adding hexagons, using the color wheel as a guide. Once hexagons are completed sew or crochet together, working through the back loops only of the stitches at the outer edge.

Happy Colors Blanket

The circles of bright colors scattered over this blanket will make you smile
every time you wrap yourself in its cozy stitches.

YOU WILL NEED

Sport-weight cotton yarn (approx 1.76 oz/
50 g; 176 yds/161 m)
MC   15 balls in white
CC   Approx 2,800 yds/2,560 m total
            of assorted colors
Size E-4 (3.5mm) hook

Gauge
A small square measures 2¾" square
A large square measures 5¼" square

Dimensions
39" x 63"

To make the blanket

For the small circles, the first three
rounds are crocheted with different
shades of the same color; for the
large circles, four shades of the same
color have been used. Start with pale
colors at the center, moving to darker
colors at the outsides.

SMALL CIRCLE-IN-SQUARE MOTIF (MAKE 254)

Using lightest shade of color of
choice, make magic loop.

Round 1: ch3 (counts as first st),
dc11 into ring, sl st into top of ch3
at beg of round. (12sts)
Fasten off yarn and join in next
shade of same color. Pull magic loop
tight to close.

Round 2: ch3 (counts as first st),
dc1 into same place as ch3 just
worked, dc2 into each st to end, sl
st into top of ch3 at beg of round.
(24sts)
Fasten off yarn and join in next

shade of same color.

Round 3: ch3 (counts as first st),
dc2 into next st, *dc1 into next st,
dc2 into next st, rep from * to end,
sl st into top of ch3 at beg of round.
(36sts)
Fasten off yarn and join in MC to
any st from last round.

EDGING

Round 4: ch1 (counts as first st),
sc1 into next 2sts, *hdc1 into next
st, dc1 into next st, work [tr1, ch1,
tr1] into next st, dc1 into next st,
hdc1 into next st, sc1 into next 4sts,
rep from *, ending last rep after two
of the sc4 have been worked, sl st
into ch1 at beg of round. (40sts)
Round 5: ch3 (counts as first st),
*dc1 into each st up to ch1sp, work
[dc2, ch1, dc2] into ch1sp, rep
from * until four ch1sp have been
worked into, dc1 into each st to
end, sl st into top of ch3 at beg of
round. (56sts)

Fasten off yarn and weave in loose ends.

LARGE CIRCLE IN SQUARE MOTIF (MAKE 23)

Work Rounds 1–3 as given for small circle, working first two rounds in lightest shade and third round in next shade of same color.

Round 4: ch3 (counts as first st), dc1 into next st, dc2 into next st, *dc1 into next 2sts, dc2 into next st, rep from * to end, sl st into top of ch3 at beg of round. (48sts)

Fasten off yarn and join in next shade of same color.

Round 5: ch3 (counts as first st), dc1 into next 2sts, dc2 into next st, *dc1 into next 3sts, dc2 into next st, rep from * to end, sl st into top of ch3 at beg of round. (60sts)

Round 6: ch3 (counts as first st), dc1 into next 3sts, dc2 into next st, *dc1 into next 4sts, dc2 into next st, rep from * to end, sl st into top of ch3 at beg of round. (72sts)

Fasten off yarn and join in next shade of same color.

Round 7: ch3 (counts as first st), dc1 into next 4sts, dc2 into next st, *dc1 into next 5sts, dc2 into next st, rep from * to end, sl st into top of ch3 at beg of round. (84sts)

Fasten off yarn and join in MC to any st from last round.

EDGING

Round 8: ch1 (counts as first st), sc1 into next 3sts, *hdc1 into next 2sts, dc1 into next 2sts, tr1 into next 2sts, work [dtr1, ch1, dtr1] into next st, tr1 into next 2sts, dc1 into next 2sts, hdc1 into next 2sts, sc1 into next 8sts, rep from *, ending last rep after four of the sc8 have been worked, sl st into ch1 at beg of round. (88sts)

Round 9: ch3 (counts as first st), *dc1 into each st up to ch1sp, work [dc2, tr1, ch1, tr1, dc2] into ch1sp, rep from * until four ch1sp have been worked into, dc1 into each st to end, sl st into top of ch3 at beg of round. (112sts)

Finishing

Using the picture as a guide, start by making larger blocks by sewing two smaller blocks to one side of a larger block, and three smaller blocks to the top or bottom of the larger block. Once you have made enough blocks for your blanket, either sew or crochet these together, making sure that you turn the blocks so you don't get a line of larger blocks.

Border

Join in MC to any stitch.

Round 1: ch1 (counts as first st), work sc1 into each st up to first ch1sp, work [sc3 into ch1sp], *sc1 into each st to next ch1sp, [sc3 into next ch1sp], rep from * until all four corners have been worked, sc1 into each st to end, sl st into ch1 at beg of round.

Round 2: ch3 (counts as first st), *work dc1 into each st up to center st of sc3 of previous round, dc3 into next st, rep from * until all four corners have been worked, dc1 into each st to end, sl st into top of ch3 at beg of round.

Fasten off yarn and weave in loose ends.

Bright colors work like a ray of sunshine, illuminating their surroundings. But the squares could be made using pastel shades for a more restful, but equally beautiful, design.

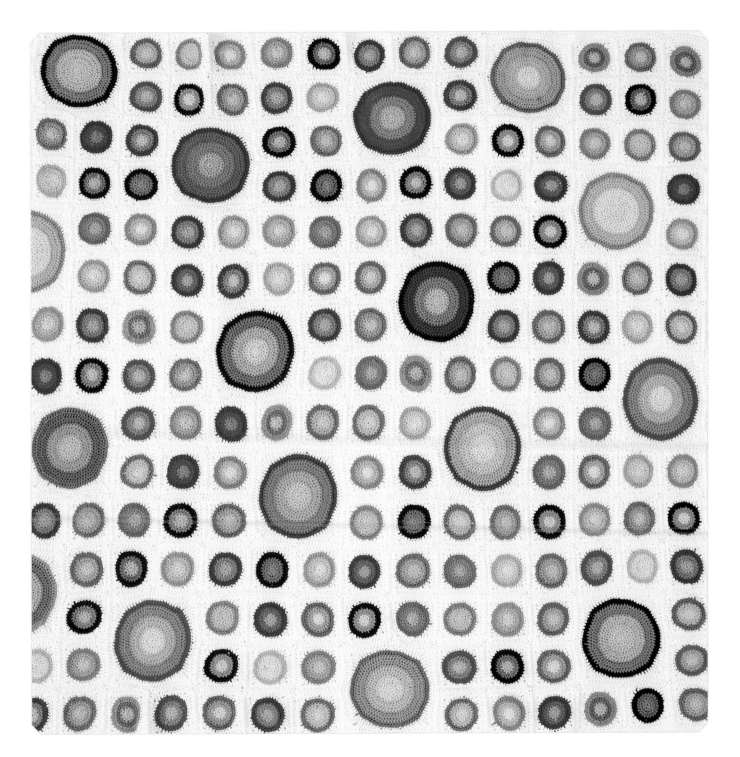

Flower Power Runner

The blooms on this open-work runner will add a shot of color to any room. Drape it over the arm or back of a sofa or chair, or arrange it on the center of a table.

YOU WILL NEED

Aran-weight cotton yarn (approx 1.76 oz/ 50 g; 83 yds/75 m)
MC   1 ball in vanilla
CC   Scraps of yarn in 15 assorted colors
Size G-6 (4mm) hook

Gauge
A flower measures 2¾" square

Dimensions
30¾" x 20½"

To make the blanket

THE FIRST FLOWER
Using MC, ch4, join ends with sl st to form ring.
Round 1: ch1, sc8 into ring, sl st into ch1 at beg of round. (8sts) Fasten off yarn and join in color of choice.
Round 2: *ch8, sl st into next st, rep from * to end, working last sl st into ch1 at beg of round. (8 loops)
Round 3: sc9 into first ch8 loop, sl st into next st, *sc9 into next ch8 loop, sl st into next st, rep from * to end.
Fasten off yarn.

SECOND FLOWER
Work Rounds 1–2 as for first flower. Join flowers together on the next round as follows.
Round 3: work [sc4 into first ch8 loop, sc1 into fifth sc of first flower petal, sc4 into ch8 loop of second flower, sl st into next st] twice, *sc9 into next ch8 loop, sl st into next st, rep from * to end.
Fasten off yarn.

THIRD FLOWER
Work as given for second flower, joining fifth and sixth petals to first and second petals of previous flower. Continue working in this way until twelve flowers have been linked. First row of runner is now complete.

FIRST FLOWER OF SECOND ROW
Work as given for second flower, joining seventh and eighth petals to third and fourth petals of twelfth flower from first row.

SECOND FLOWER OF SECOND ROW
Work as given for second flower, joining fifth and sixth petals to first and second petals of previous flower and seventh and eight petals to third and forth petals from eleventh flower from first row.

Continue working in this way until
twelve flowers have been linked.
Second row is now complete.
Link a further six rows of flowers.

Finishing
Weave in loose ends and block if
required.

Star Fruit Rug

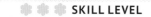

SKILL LEVEL

Bold colors bring a modern, boho touch to the star motifs on this rug. The stars are crocheted together as you work in a series of progressive sets of colors.

YOU WILL NEED

Worsted/aran-weight wool yarn (approx 3.5 oz/100 g; 155 yds/142 m)

CC	1 skein in orange red
CCa	1 skein in red
CCb	1 skein in gold
CCc	1 skein in light green
CCd	1 skein in medium green
CCe	1 skein in turquoise
CCf	1 skein in light blue
CCg	1 skein in magenta
CCh	1 skein in dark blue

Size G-6 (4mm) hook

Gauge
A star motif measures approx 4" across from point to point

Dimensions
Approx 37" x 24"

Special stitches
FPdc and FPtr: dc and tr, respectively, worked behind the post of the designated stitch on the side facing you.

Surface sl st: insert hook through designated st and draw up loop from the WS of the motif and complete sl st on the RS; insert hook into next designated st, draw up loop, and complete sl st. Continue around the motif working into each designated st.

NOTE: each star motif requires approximately 17 yards of worsted/aran-weight yarn. If you choose to design something with different dimensions, multiply the total number of motifs by 17 yards to determine the total length of yarn required. For example, if you want to make a rug measuring 37" x 48", you will need 2 skeins of each color.

To make the rug
FIRST STAR MOTIF
First Motif

Using color of choice, ch6, join ends with sl st to form ring.

Round 1: *ch1, work [dc1, tr1, dc1, ch1, sl st] into ring, ch1, rep from * 5 more times. (6 petals)

Round 2: *ch2, skip ch1, work [FPdc into next st, FPtr into next st, FPdc into next st, ch2], skip ch1, sl st into sl st from previous round, rep from * to end.

Round 3: *ch2, skip ch2, work [FPdc into next st, FPtr into next st, FPdc into next st, ch2], skip ch2, sc1 into sl st from previous round, rep from * to end.

Fasten off yarn and weave in loose ends.

NOTE: the next round is worked using the surface crochet technique and a contrasting color. The hook is used with the RS of the motif facing, but the yarn will be held at the WS of the motif.

Work the surface sl st around motif, inserting hook into the top of each designated st or sp below.

Round 4: Join contrast color with sl st into final sc of Round 3, then work down toward the center of the motif as follows, working down the edge of the last of the six petals. Sl st into corresponding sp on Round 2, sl st into corresponding st of Round 1, sl st into center of ring, *work sl st into each sp back up the right side of next petal, ending with sl st into ch2sp, sl st into blo of next 3sts**, work sl st into each sp back down left-hand side of same petal, and into loop, rep from *, ending last rep at **.

Fasten off yarn and pull tail through to WS. Weave in loose ends.

NOTE: the next round is worked into the top of the sts from Round 3; they are at the WS of the motif.

Round 5: join next color into any sl st on Round 3, *sl st into ch2sp, sc1 into next st, work [sc1, ch3, sc1] into next st (corner worked), sc1 into next st, sl st into next ch2sp, rep from * to end, sl st into sl st at beg of round.

SECOND STAR MOTIF

Using next set of three colors, start by working Rounds 1–4 as given for first motif.

NOTE: you will also join the motifs together as you go on next round.

Round 5: join next color into any sl st on Round 3, *sl st into next ch2sp, sc1 into next st, work [sc1, ch1, sl st into ch3sp from first motif, ch1, sc1] into next st (corner join worked), sc1 into next st, sl st into next ch2sp, rep from *, working corner join into two corners only for first row of motifs, for remaining corners work as Round 5 of first motif.

Using picture as a guide, join all the motifs together as Round 5, working into two corners from each motif.

Finishing

Work a total of seven rows, maintaining the progressive sequence of colors as shown in the picture. Weave in loose ends and block if required.

Each star fruit motif uses three colors. Create multiple color combinations and maximum color contrast.

Large Granny-Square Pillow

Brightly colored cotton yarns make a pillow ideal for sunny days.
Make a couple for your sofa or a set to use in the garden.

YOU WILL NEED

Scraps of DK-weight cotton yarn in
8 assorted colors
18" x 18" pillow in plain, neutral color
Size G-6 (4mm) hook

Gauge

Each pattern repeat triangle measures
approx ¾" wide at the base
Approx 8 rows of 4 pattern repeats per
4" square

Dimensions

To fit 18" square pillow form

Pictured on page 35, top

To make the pillow

Using color of choice, ch5, join ends
with sl st to form ring.

Round 1: ch3 (counts as first dc),
dc2 into ring, *ch3, dc3 into ring,
rep from * twice more, ch3, sl st
into top of ch3 at beg of round.
(4 sets of dc3)
Fasten off yarn and join new color
into any ch3sp.

Round 2: ch3 (counts as first dc),
work [dc2, ch3, dc3] into same
ch3sp, *ch1, skip next 3sts, work
[dc3, ch3, dc3] into next ch3sp, rep
from * twice more, ch1, sl st into
top of ch3 at beg of round.
(8 sets of dc3)
Fasten off yarn and join new color
into any ch3sp.

Round 3: ch3 (counts as first dc),
work [dc2, ch3, dc3] into same
ch3sp, *ch1, skip next 3sts, dc3 in
ch1sp, ch1**, work [dc3, ch3, dc3]
into next ch3sp, rep from * 3 more
times, ending last rep at **, sl st into

top of ch3 at beg of round.
(12 sets of dc3)
Fasten off yarn and join new color
into any ch3sp.

Round 4: ch3 (counts as first dc),
work [dc2, ch3, dc3] into same
ch3sp, *[ch1, skip next 3sts, dc3
into ch1sp, ch1] twice**, work [dc3,
ch3, dc3] into next ch3sp, rep from
* 3 more times, ending last rep at **,
sl st into top of ch3 at beg of round.
(16 sets of dc3)
Fasten off yarn and join new color
into any ch3sp.

Repeat Round 4, keeping increases
as set, adding one set of dc3 to each
of the side sections until approx 17
rounds have been worked or panel
measures approx 17" x 17".

Edging

Using color of choice, join yarn into top of any dc of Round 4.

Round 5: ch1, sc1 into same st, work sc1 into each st and ch1sp, work sc3 into each ch3sp, sl st into ch1 at beg of round. Fasten off yarn.

Finishing

Block panel to correct size and weave in loose ends.

Pin crochet panel to pillow, then using a sharp sewing needle and matching thread, sew into place.

Sunflower Motif Pillow

Simple granny squares build up to make a colorful, cozy pillow. Raid your yarn stash
for the motif colors and choose a border color to contrast or complement them.

YOU WILL NEED

DK-weight cotton/bamboo blend yarn
(approx 3.5 oz/100 g; 250 yds/230 m)
MC   1 ball in cream
Scraps of yarn in 4 colors for the motifs
18" x 18" pillow form
Size E-4 (3.5mm) hook

Gauge
Each granny square measures approx
3½" square

Dimensions
To fit 18" square pillow form

To make the pillow

GRANNY SQUARE MOTIF (MAKE 16)
Using color of choice, make magic
loop.

Round 1: ch3 (counts as first dc),
dc11 into loop, join with sl st into
top of ch3 at beg of round. (12dc)
Fasten off yarn and join in color
of choice in between any of the
stitches.

Round 2: ch3 (counts as first dc),
dc1 into same sp, *dc2 into next sp,
rep from * to end, sl st into top of
ch3 at beg of round.
(12 sets of dc2)
Fasten off yarn and join in color of
choice in between any of the sets
of dc2.

Round 3: ch3 (counts as first dc),
dc2 into same sp, skip next 2sts,
*dc3 into next sp, skip next 2sts, rep
from * to end, sl st into top of ch3 at
beg of round. (12 sets of dc3)
Fasten off yarn and join in MC in
between any of the sets of dc3.

Round 4: ch3 (counts as first dc),
work [dc2, ch2, dc3] into same sp,
*work [skip 3sts, dc3 into next sp]
twice, skip 3sts**, work [dc3, ch2,
dc3] into next sp, rep from * 3 more
times, ending last rep at **, sl st into
top of ch3 at beg of round.

Round 5: ch1 (counts as first sc),
sc1 into next 2sts, work sc3 into first
ch2sp (first corner made), *sc1 into
each st to next ch2sp, work sc3 into
next ch2sp (corner made), rep from
* twice more, sc1 into each st to
end, sl st into ch1 at beg of round.
Fasten off yarn. Weave in loose ends.
Make a further 15 squares.

Finishing
Sew the squares together to make
four rows of four squares.

Edging

Using MC and with RS facing, join yarn to any stitch on outer edge.

Round 1: ch3 (counts as first dc), dc1 into each st to corner, *work [dc2, ch2, dc2] into next st (corner made), dc1 into each st to next corner, rep from * until four corners have been made, dc1 into each st to end, sl st into top of ch3 at beg of round.

Repeat Round 1 until work is required size, working [dc2, ch2, dc2] into each ch2sp to make corners.

Fasten off yarn and weave in loose ends.

Block the panel so it is square. Pin crochet panel to pillow, then using sharp sewing needle and matching thread, sew into place.

Chevron Pillow

〰〰〰〰〰〰〰〰〰〰〰〰〰〰〰〰〰〰〰〰〰〰〰〰

✤ ✤ **SKILL LEVEL**

Alternating cream and colored chevrons make a smart cover for a pillow. To make using different colors easier, use a separate ball of yarn for each chevron.

YOU WILL NEED

Aran-weight cotton yarn (approx 1.76 oz/ 50 g; 83 yds/75 m)

MC	5 balls in off white
CCa	1 ball in gold
CCb	1 ball in vanilla
CCc	1 ball in rust
CCd	1 ball in light blue
CCe	1 ball in medium blue
CCf	1 ball in dark beige
CCg	1 ball in light pink
CCh	1 ball in moss green

16" x 16" pillow form
4 buttons, 1" diameter
Size G-6 (4mm) hook

Gauge
A chevron measures 3¼" x 2"

Dimensions
To fit 16" square pillow form

To make the pillow
Using MC, ch72.

Row 1: dc2 into 3rd ch from hook, dc1 into next ch3, work [dc3tog over next ch3] twice, dc1 into next ch3, dc3 into next st, *change to CC of choice, dc3 into next ch, dc1 into next ch3, work [dc3tog over next ch3] twice, dc1 into next ch3, dc3 into next ch, change to MC, dc3 into next ch, dc1 into next ch3, work [dc3tog over next ch3] twice, dc1 into next ch3, dc3 into next ch, rep from * once more, turn. (5 chevrons) Keeping chevron block colors correct as set, work next row as follows.

Row 2: ch2 (counts as first dc), dc2 into st, *dc1 into next 3sts, work [dc3tog over next 3sts] twice, dc1 into next 3sts**, work [dc3 into next st] twice, rep from * 4 more times, ending last rep at **, work dc3 into top of ch2 at beg of previous row, turn.

Row 2 forms chevron pattern; repeat Row 2 twice more. Fasten off yarn.

Row 5: work as Row 2 starting with CC of choice, then MC.

Repeat Row 5 three more times. Fasten off yarn.

Keeping chevron block pattern as set, repeat until 16 sets of the four-row chevrons have been worked. On last row of final chevron do not fasten off yarn; join in MC for button band.

To make the buttonholes

Row 1: ch2 (counts as first dc), dc2 into first st, *dc1 into next 3sts, work [dc3tog over next 3sts] twice, dc1 into next 3sts**, ch3, skip 2sts, rep from * 4 more times, ending last rep at **, dc3 into top of ch2 at beg of previous row, turn.

Row 2: ch2 (counts as first dc), dc2 into first st, dc1 into next 3sts, *work [dc3tog over next 3sts] twice, dc1 into next st, dc8 into ch3sp,

dc1 into next st, rep from * 3 more times, work [dc3tog over next 3sts] twice, dc1 into next 3sts, dc3 into top of ch2 at beg of previous row. Fasten off yarn and weave in loose ends.

Finishing
Block the fabric. With WS facing, make an envelope by folding the plain edge over the buttonholed edge. Make sure that the length of your folded cover measures the same as the width to make it approx 16" square. Sew down the sides of the cover using matching yarn and backstitch. Turn RS out, making sure the corners are pointed (use a pencil to push the corner out), then sew buttons onto the plain edge to correspond with the buttonholes. Insert pillow form.

Use the photographs as a guide for placing the contrast colors, or make up your own color pattern.

Round Floor Pillow

Simple rounds of double crochet quickly build up into a cover for a circular pillow. The pattern is easy to adapt for any size of pillow insert—just add or subtract rounds.

YOU WILL NEED

Scraps of sport-weight cotton yarn in 7 assorted colors
14"-diameter circular pillow form
Size G-6 (4mm) hook

Gauge
21 stitches by 11 rows over 4" square using dc

Dimensions
To fit a 14"-diameter pillow form

To make the pillow

FRONT PANEL

Using color of choice, ch4, join ends with sl st to form ring.

Round 1: ch4 (counts as dc1 and ch1), *dc1 into ring, ch1, rep from * 6 more times, sl st into third of ch4 at beg of round. (8 spaces)
Fasten off yarn and join color of choice into first ch1sp.

Round 2: ch3 (counts as first dc), dc1 into same ch1sp, ch1, *dc2 into next ch1sp, ch1, rep from * to end, sl st into top of ch3 at beg of round.
Fasten off yarn and join color of choice into first ch1sp.

Round 3: ch3 (counts as first dc), work [dc1, ch1, dc2] into same ch1sp, *work [dc2, ch1, dc2] into each ch1sp, ch1, rep from * to end, sl st into top of ch3 at beg of round. (8 sets of dc2, ch1, dc2)
Fasten off yarn and join color of choice into first ch1sp.

Round 4: ch3 (counts as first dc), dc1 into same ch1sp, ch1, *dc2 into next ch1sp, ch1, rep from * to end, sl st into top of ch3 at beg of round. (16 sets of dc2)
Fasten off yarn and join in color of choice.

Round 5: ch3 (counts as first dc), dc1 into next st, work dc1 into each st and ch1sp to end, sl st into top of ch3 at beg of round. (48sts)
Fasten off yarn and join in color of choice.

Round 6: ch3 (counts as first dc), dc1 into next 2sts, dc2 into next st, *dc1 into next 3sts, dc2 into next st, rep from * to end, sl st into top of ch3 at beg of round. (60sts)
Fasten off yarn and join in color of choice.

Round 7: ch3 (counts as first dc), dc1 into next 3sts, dc2 into next st, *dc1 into next 4sts, dc2 into next st, rep from * to end, sl st into top of ch3 at beg of round. (72sts)

Fasten off yarn and join in color of choice.

Round 8: ch3 (counts as first dc), dc1 into next 4sts, dc2 into next st, *dc1 into next 5sts, dc2 into next st, rep from * to end, sl st into top of ch3 at beg of round. (84sts)
Fasten off yarn and join in color of choice.

Round 9: ch3 (counts as first dc), dc1 into next 5sts, dc2 into next st, *dc1 into next 6sts, dc2 into next st, rep from * to end, sl st into top of ch3 at beg of round. (96sts)
Keeping pattern and increasing as set, continue working until you have 240sts.
To ensure a snug fit, make sure the panel is slightly smaller than pillow form. Fasten off yarn and weave in loose ends.

> *This comfortable floor pillow is the perfect seat, whether you want to watch television, have a picnic in the garden, or enjoy a good book.*

Back panel

Using color of choice, ch4, join ends with sl st to form ring.

Round 1: ch3 (counts as first dc), dc11 into ring, sl st into top of ch3 at beg of round. (12sts)
Fasten off yarn and join in color of choice.

Round 2: ch3 (counts as first dc), dc1 into same place as base of ch3, *dc2 into next st, rep from * to end, sl st into top of ch3 at beg of round. (24sts)
Fasten off yarn and join in color of choice.

Round 3: ch3 (counts as first dc), dc2 into first st, *dc1 into next st, dc2 into next st, rep from * to end, sl st into top of ch3 at beg of round. (36sts)
Fasten off yarn and join in color of choice.

Round 4: ch3, (counts as first dc), dc1 into next st, dc2 into next st, *dc1 into next 2sts, dc2 into next st, rep from * to end, sl st into ch3 at beg of round. (48sts)
Fasten off yarn and join in color of choice.

Round 5: ch3 (counts as first dc), dc1 into next 2sts, dc2 into next st, *dc1 into next 3sts, dc2 into next st, rep from * to end, sl st into top of ch3 at beg of round. (60sts)
Keeping pattern and increasing as set, continue working until back panel matches front panel. Fasten off yarn and weave in loose ends.

Finishing

Sew front and back panels together as follows: place the panels together with RS facing outwards, then sew halfway around the outer edge, working through the top of the stitches. Insert the pillow form, then continue working around the outer edge. Weave in loose ends.

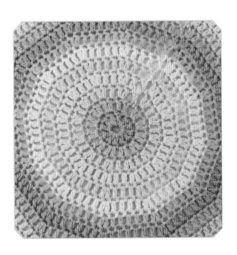

Spoke Mandala

Crocheted mandalas—colorful disks often used as wall decorations—were originally symbolic pictures of the universe used in Tibetan Buddhism. They were designed to represent an imaginary palace that is contemplated during meditation. Each section has its own significance, representing an aspect of wisdom or reminding the meditator of a guiding principle. Many crocheters find making mandalas a therapeutic experience.

YOU WILL NEED

Scraps of worsted-weight cotton yarn in 8 assorted colors
Size G-6 (4mm) crochet hook
Size G-6 (4mm) Tunisian crochet hook
Tapestry needle

Gauge

Gauge is not important in this project

Dimensions

8¼" diameter

Special stitches

Standing dc: place slipknot on hook, yo, insert hook into st, yo and draw through (3 loops on hook), yo and draw through first two loops (2 loops on hook), yo and draw through last two loops (1 loop on hook).

To make the mandala

Using G-6 hook and color of choice, make magic loop.

Round 1: ch2 (counts as first dc), dc11 into loop. (12dc)

Pull magic loop tight to close ring. Break off yarn and pull through the loop on your hook.

Close round as follows on this and every following round.

Thread yarn through the tapestry needle and insert in the first dc you made under both loops. Pull the needle through, then insert the needle from the front to the back of the back loop of the last stitch you made. Pull the yarn gently to close round.

Join in color of choice into blo of first stitch of previous round using standing dc technique (counts as first st).

Round 2: dc1 into blo of same st as standing dc, dc2 into blo of each st to end. (24sts)

Close round as before.

Join in color of choice into first stitch of previous round using standing dc technique (counts as first st).

Round 3: dc2 into next st, *dc1 into next st, dc2 into next st, rep from * to end. (36sts)

Close round as before.

Join in color of choice into first stitch

of previous round using standing dc technique (counts as first st).

Round 4: dc1 into next st, dc2 into next st, *dc1 into next 2sts, dc2 into next st, rep from * to end. (48sts)
Close round as before.

Join in color of choice into first stitch of previous round using standing dc technique (counts as first st).

Round 5: dc1 into next 2sts, dc2 into next st, *dc1 into next 3sts, dc2 into next st, rep from * to end. (60sts)
Close round as before.

Join in color of choice into first stitch of previous round using standing dc technique (counts as first st).

Round 6: dc1 into next 3sts, dc2 into next st, *dc1 into next 4sts, dc2 into next st, rep from * to end. (72sts)
Close round as before.

Join in color of choice into first stitch of previous round using standing dc technique (counts as first st).

Round 7: dc1 into next 4sts, dc2 into next st, *dc1 into next 5sts, dc2 into next st, rep from * to end. (84sts)
Close round as before.

To make the wedges

Join in color of choice into first st—do not use standing dc technique.

Round 8: ch1, sc1 into same st, *skip next 2sts, dc6 into next st, skip next 2sts, sc1 into next st, rep from * to end. (14 wedges)
Close round as before.

To make the spokes

Using G-6 Tunisian hook, insert hook into blo of third dc of any wedge and join in color of choice. Extended stitches are worked into the front loops from Round 1; two of the extended stitches will need to be worked into the same front loop. Work all stitches (except extended stitches) in this round into back loops only.

Round 9: sc1 into next st, hdc1 into next 2sts, dc1 into next st, make extended st as follows [yo] 10 times (11 loops on hook), insert hook into corresponding front loop from Round 1, *yo and draw through 2 loops, rep from * until 1 loop left on hook], **hdc1 into next 2sts, sc1 into next 2sts, hdc1 into next 2sts, dc1 into next st, make extended st as before, rep from ** until 14 extended sts have been worked, hdc1 into next st, sc1 into last st. (14 extended sts)
Close round as before.

Finishing

Using G-6 hook and same color as previous round, join into first stitch of previous round using standing dc technique (counts as first st).

Round 10: dc1 into each st to end. (98sts)

Fasten off yarn. Weave in loose ends.

Picot-Edge Mandala

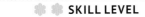 **SKILL LEVEL**

Mandalas are a great way to use up scraps of yarn. They also allow you to experiment by combining different colors to discover the effects you can create.

YOU WILL NEED

Scraps of worsted-weight cotton yarn in 12 assorted colors
Size G-6 (4mm) hook
Tapestry needle

Gauge
Gauge is not important in this project

Dimensions
12" diameter

Special stitches
Standing dc: place slipknot on hook, yo, insert hook into st, yo and draw through (3 loops on hook), yo and draw through first two loops (2 loops on hook), yo and draw through last two loops (1 loop on hook)

Pictured on page 49

To make the mandala

Using color of choice, make a magic loop.

Round 1: ch2 (counts as first dc), dc11 into ring. (12dc)

Pull magic loop tight to close ring. Break off yarn and pull through the loop on your hook. Close round as follows on every round.

Thread yarn through the tapestry needle and insert in the first dc you made under both loops.

Pull the needle through, then insert the needle from the front to the back of the back loop of the last stitch you made. Pull the yarn gently to close round.

Join in color of choice into blo of first stitch of previous round using standing dc technique (counts as first st).

Round 2: dc1 into same st as standing dc, dc2 into each st to end. (24sts)

Close round as before.

Join in color of choice into first stitch of previous round using standing dc technique (counts as first st).

Round 3: dc2 into next st, *dc1 into next st, dc2 into next st, rep from * to end. (36sts)

Close round as before.

Join in color of choice into first stitch of previous round using standing dc technique (counts as first st).

Round 4: dc1 into next st, dc2 into next st, *dc1 into next 2sts, dc2 into next st, rep from * to end. (48sts)

Close round as before.

Join in color of choice into first stitch of previous round using standing dc technique (counts as first st).

Round 5: dc1 into next 2sts, dc2 into next st, *dc1 into next 3sts, dc2 into next st, rep from * to end. (60sts)

Close round as before.

Mandalas are versatile objects–use them as wall decorations, coasters, pot holders, or to line baskets. Use a large hook and chunky yarn to make rug-sized mandalas or a slim hook and lace-weight yarn to make miniature mandalas to use as gift tags.

Join in color of choice into first stitch of previous round using standing dc technique (counts as first st).

Round 6: dc1 into next 3sts, dc2 into next st, *dc1 into next 4sts, dc2 into next st, rep from * to end. (72sts)
Close round as before.
Join in color of choice into first stitch of previous round using standing dc technique (counts as first st).

Round 7: dc1 into next 4sts, dc2 into next st, *dc1 into next 5sts, dc2 into next st, rep from * to end. (84sts)
Close round as before.
Join in color of choice into first stitch of previous round using standing dc technique (counts as first st).

Round 8: dc1 into next 5sts, dc2 into next st, *dc1 into next 6sts, dc2 into next st, rep from * to end. (96sts)
Close round as before.
Join in color of choice into first stitch of previous round using standing dc technique (counts as first st).

Round 9: dc1 into next 6sts, dc2 into next st, *dc1 into next 7sts, dc2 into next st, rep from * to end. (108sts)
Close round as before.
Join in color of choice into first stitch of previous round using standing dc technique (counts as first st).

Round 10: dc1 into next 7sts, dc2 into next st, *dc1 into next 8sts, dc2 into next st, rep from * to end. (120sts)
Close round as before.
Join in color of choice into first stitch of previous round using standing dc technique (counts as first st).

Round 11: dc1 into next 8sts, dc2 into next st, *dc1 into next 9sts, dc2 into next st, rep from * to end. (132sts)
Close round as before.
Join in color of choice into first stitch of previous round using standing dc technique (counts as first st).

To make the edging and loop
Join in color of choice to first st—do not use standing dc technique.
Round 12: ch1, sc1 into same st, *skip next 2sts, dc6 into next st, skip next 2sts, sc1 into next st, rep from * to end, sl st into ch1 at beg of round. (22 fans)
Join yarn for loop as follows: insert hook into first stitch, yo and draw through, sc1 into same st, ch10, sc1 into same st.
Fasten off yarn and weave in loose ends.

Finishing
Block if required.

The double crochet stitch is versatile, easy to master, and quick to work.

Mandala Stool Cover

A three-dimensional mandala with a teardrop edging
makes a perfect cover for a circular stool or chair seat.

YOU WILL NEED

Scraps of worsted-weight yarn

CCa	green
CCb	pink
CCc	teal
CCd	blue
CCe	yellow
CCf	red
CCg	lilac
CCh	light green
CCi	orchid
CCj	burnt orange
CCk	royal blue
CCl	violet

1 ball of worsted-weight yarn (16 oz/448 g;
1,020 yds/932 m) in antique white for
edging (CCm)

Size G-6 (4mm) hook

Tapestry needle

Gauge
4¼" diameter in pattern to Round 4B

Dimensions
To fit a 12"-diameter seat

Special stitches

Surface slip stitch (surf sl st): insert hook RS facing through designated stitch or space. Pull up loop from behind the work, insert into next st or space, pull up loop from behind, and complete slip stitch. Insert hook into next st or space and continue slip-stitching around. Fasten off. Pull ends through to back and weave in.

dc3 cluster (dc3cl): work [yo, insert hook through st, yo, pull back through st, yo, pull through 2 loops on hook] 3 times, yo, pull through all 4 loops on hook.

dc4 popcorn (dc4pop): dc4 in same st, remove hook from loop, insert hook through first dc and into loop, yo, pull through loop and st on hook.

dc3 popcorn (dc3pop): dc3 in same st, remove hook from loop, insert hook through first dc and back into loop, yo, and pull through loop and st on hook.

standing dc: place slipknot on hook, yo, insert hook into st, yo and draw through (3 loops on hook), yo and draw through first two loops (2 loops on hook), yo and draw through last two loops (1 loop on hook).

Picot: ch3, sl st in first ch.

To make the stool cover

This mandala is crocheted in the round with RS facing you. Each round is started by joining with a new color and then fastened off at the end of each round unless otherwise noted in the pattern. Join with standing stitches at the beginning of each round. Alternatively, join with a sl st and raise your stitches using chains; this will count as your first stitch.

NOTE: many of the rounds are worked in two parts; the first part of the round is indicated with A and the second part of the round or the surface embellishment with B.

Using CCj, make magic loop.

Round 1A: ch4 (counts as dc1 and ch1), *dc1 into ring, ch1, rep from * 10 more times, sl st into third of ch4 at beg of round. (12dc)

Pull magic loop tight to close ring. Break off yarn and pull through loop on your hook. Close round as follows on this and every following round. Thread yarn through the tapestry needle and insert in the first dc you made under both loops. Pull the needle through, then insert the needle from the front to the back of the back loop of the last stitch you made.

Pull the yarn gently to close round.

Round 1B: Using CCb, work a surface sl st between the posts of the stitches of round just worked, join with sl st into first sl st. (12sl sts)

Break off yarn and close round as before.

Using standing dc technique, join CCe into any of the ch1sp of Round 1A (counts as first st).

Round 2A: ch1, *dc1 into next ch1sp, ch1, rep from * to end. Break off yarn and close as before. The next round is worked into the top of the stitches from Round 1A, behind the stitches of the round just worked.

Using standing dc technique, join yarn CCf into any of the stitches from Round 1A (counts as first st).

Round 2B: ch1, *dc1 into next st, ch1, rep from * to end. Break off yarn and close as before. The next round is worked into the

Add or subtract rounds from the pattern to create a mandala cover to fit your stool.

ch1sp of Rounds 2A and 2B.

Using standing dc technique, join CCm into any of the ch1sp from Rounds 2A and 2B (counts as first st).

Round 3A: dc2 into same ch1sp, ch1, *dc3 into next ch1sp, ch1, rep from * to end. (12 sets of dc3) Close round as before.

Round 3B: Using CCa, work a surface sl st between each stitch of round just worked, join with sl st into first sl st. (36 sl sts)

Using standing dc technique, join CCd into any of the ch1sp from Round 3A (counts as first st).

Round 4A: dc2cl into same ch1sp, ch3, *dc3cl into next ch1sp, ch3, rep from * to end. (12 dc3cl) Close round as before.

This next round is worked into Round 4A and Round 3A.

Join CCc into the left-hand side of any of the ch3sp next to a dc3cl with a sl st.

Round 4B: sc1 into ch3sp, *sc1 into top of dc3cl, sc1 into next ch3sp, work [dc4pop] into center stitch of dc3 from Round 3A, sc1 into same ch3sp, rep from * to end. Close round as before.

Join CCm into top of any of the dc4pop from Round 4B with a sl st.

Round 5: sc1 into same st as sl st, ch4, *sc1 into top of next dc4pop, ch4, rep from * to end. Close round as before.

Join CCk using standing dc technique into any of the ch4sp from Round 5 (counts as first st).

Round 6A: dc4 into same ch4sp, ch1, *dc5 into next ch4sp, ch1, rep from * to end. (12 sets of dc5) Close round as before.

Round 6B: Using CCh, work a surface sl st into top of each st and ch1sp of Round 6A, join with sl st into first sl st. (72sts)

This next round is worked into the top of the stitches from Round 6A behind the sl sts from Round 6B. Join CCg into ch1sp from Round 6A using standing dc technique (counts as first st).

Round 7A: ch3, *skip next 2sts, dc1 into next st, ch3, skip next 2sts, dc1 into next ch1sp, ch3, rep from * 10 more times, skip next 2sts, dc1 into next st, skip next 2sts, ch3, sl st into top of first st.

Do not break off yarn.

This next round is worked around the posts of stitches from Round 7A to create a wave effect.

Round 7B: *With RS facing, work dc5 around post of next st, then dc5 around post of next st back up toward outer edge, rep from * to end.

Close round as before.

This next round is worked into the ch3sp from Round 7A.

Join CCi with sl st into any of the ch3sp from Round 7A.

Round 8: *work [sc1, hdc1, dc1, hdc1, sc1] into next ch3sp (scallop worked), rep from * to end. (24 scallops)

Close round as before.

Join CCl into sc1 at the right-hand side of any of the scallops using standing dc technique (counts as first st).

Round 9A: dc1 into next st, ch4, *skip next 3sts, dc1 into next 2sts, ch4, rep from * to end.
Close round as before.
The next round is worked into the sts of Round 9A and around the posts of stitches in Round 8 behind the ch4sp.
Join CCm with sl st into first of the dc2 on Round 9A.
Round 9B: *sc1 into each of the next 2sts of Round 9A, then work FPdc1 into next st of Round 8 scallop, FPdc2 into next st, FPdc1 into next st, rep from * to end.
Close round as before.
The next round is worked into the top of the sts from Round 9B and the ch4sp of Round 9A.
Join CCj using standing dc technique into first of dc2 in Round 9B (counts as first st).
Round 10A: dc1 into next st, sc1 into next ch4sp from Round 9A, *dc2 into next 2sts from Round 9B, sc1 into next ch4sp from Round 9A, rep from * to end.
Close round as before.
The next round is worked into the top and around the base of the sts from Round 10A.
Join CCb into the right-hand side of sc1 from Round 10A.
Round 10B: ch5, *sl st in between next 2sts, sl st into base of next 4sts

from Round 10A, sl st into space at the left-hand side of next st**, ch5, rep from *, ending last rep at **. Close round as before.

The next round is worked into the top of the stitches from Round 10A and the popcorns are worked into the st to the back of the ch5 loops of Round 10B.

{ *Make time to check the stitches you are working into on each round.*

Join CCe into blo of first dc stitch from Round 10A with a sl st.

Round 11: *sc1 into blo of next 4sts, dc3pop into next st, push popcorn just worked through the ch5 loop from Round 10B, rep from * to end. (24 popcorns)
Close round as before.

The next round is worked into the blo of stitches on Round 11 and the back loop of center ch of ch5 from round 10B.

Join CCf into back of third ch of ch5 from Round 10B and popcorn from Round 11.

Round 12A: skip next st, *dc4 into blo of next 2sts, skip next st**, sl st into third of next ch5 and back of next popcorn, rep from *, ending last rep at **. (24 scallops)
Close round as before.

Join CCa with sl st into top of popcorn join from Round 12A.

Round 12B: *sl st in between the next 4 st posts from the row below, ch3, sl st into base of ch just worked (picot made), sl st into next 4stsp, rep from * to end. (24 picots)
Close round as before.

Mandala stool top section is now complete. Fasten off yarn and weave in loose ends.

Edging
Join CCm into blo of st behind picot with sl st.
Work into blo for these next rounds throughout.

Round 13: *hdc1 into next 2sts, dc1 into next st, dc2tog working first dc into next st, skip sl st, and work second dc into next st, dc1 into next st, hdc1 into next 2sts, sl st into back of next picot, rep from * to end, sl st into sl st at beg of round.

Round 14: ch3 (counts as first st), skip next st, dc1 into next 5sts, dc2tog over next st and sl st behind picot, *dc1 into next 6sts, dc2tog over next st and picot, rep from *

to end, sl st into top ch3 at beg of round. (24 decreases)

Round 15: ch3 (counts as first st), dc1 into each st to first decrease, dc3pop into next st, *dc1 into each st to next decrease, dc3pop into next st, rep from * to end, sl st into top of ch3 at beg of round. (24 popcorns)

Round 16: ch3 (counts as first st), dc1 into each st to end, sl st into top of ch3 at beg of round.

Round 17: ch3, dc1 into next 2sts, *skip next st, FPdc1 around next st, FPdc1 around skipped st, dc1 into next 5sts, rep from *, ending last rep with dc1 into last 2sts, sl st into top of ch3 at beg of round.

Round 18: ch3 (counts as first st), dc2 into same place as join, skip next 2sts, *dc3 into next st, skip 2sts, rep from * to end, sl st into top of ch3 at beg of round. (56 dc3)

Round 19: *ch3, skip next 3sts, sl st in between next 2sts, rep from * to end, sl st into top of ch3 at beg of round. (56 ch3)

Round 20: work [sc1, hdc1, dc1, hdc1, sc1] into each ch3sp to end, sl st into sc1 at beg of round.

Finishing
Fasten off and weave in ends.

Heart and Flower Motifs

Pretty heart and flower motifs are a great way to use up scraps of yarn to make individual decorations or to complete the wreath shown on page 59. Work each flower as given in different color combinations.

YOU WILL NEED

Scraps of sport-weight cotton yarn in variety of colors
Size C-2 (2.75mm) hook

Gauge
Gauge is not important in this project

Dimensions
Daisy approx 2¼" x 2¼"
Heart approx 2½" high

To make a heart (see page 58, top)

Using MC of choice, ch2.
Row 1: sc3 into 2nd ch from hook, turn. (3sts)
Row 2: ch1, sc2 into first st, sc1 into next st, sc2 into last st, turn. (5sts)
Row 3: ch1, sc2 into first st, sc1 into next 3sts, sc2 into last st, turn. (7sts)
Rows 4–6: ch1, sc1 into each st to end, turn.
Row 7: sl st into first st, dc5 into next st, sl st into next 3sts, dc5 into next st, sl st into last st, do not turn (10sts)
With RS facing, continue in rounds as follows.
Round 8: ch1, work sc5 down toward point, work [sc1, hdc1, sc1] into point, work sc8 evenly up the side until you reach the third st of the dc5 from previous row, work sc3 into next st, sc1 into next 2sts, sl st into next st, skip next st, sl st into next st, sc1 into next 2sts, sc3 into next st, sc1 into next 3sts, sl st into ch1 at beg of round. (28sts)
Fasten off yarn and join in CC to any stitch from previous round.
Work into each stitch as follows:
*ch2, sl st into next st, rep from * to end.
Fasten off yarn and weave in loose ends.

To make a daisy (see page 58, center)

Using color of choice, ch4 (counts as ch1 and dc1).
Round 1: dc11 into 4th ch from hook, sl st into top of initial ch4. (12sts)
Fasten off yarn and join in color of choice to any st from previous round.
Round 2: ch1, sc1 into same st as you joined yarn into, sc2 into next st, *sc1 into next st, sc2 into next st, rep from * to end, sl st into ch1 at beg of round. (18sts)

Glue or stitch the flowers to an embroidery hoop to make a summery wreath. The possibilities for making motifs are endless: substitute colors, layer motifs, extend the patterns to make more rounds, or add a couple of chain stitches between the outer double crochet stitches to make pointed rather than round petal shapes.

Fasten off yarn and join in color of choice to any st from previous round.
Round 3: ch2, dc1 into same st, dc1 into next st, *ch2, sl st into next st, ch2, dc1 into same st as sl st just worked, dc1 into next st, rep from * to end, ch2, sl st into base of ch2 at beg of round. (9 petals)
Fasten off yarn and weave in loose ends. Block if required.

To make seven-petal flower (see below left)
Using color of choice, ch4 (counts as ch1 and dc1).
Round 1: dc13 into 4th ch from hook, sl st into top of initial ch4. (14sts)
Fasten off yarn and join in color of choice to any st from previous round.
Round 2: ch1, sc1 into same st as you joined yarn into, sc2 into next st, *sc1 into next st, sc2 into next st,

rep from * to end, sl st into ch1 at beg of round. (21sts)
Fasten off yarn and join in color of choice to any st from previous round.
Round 3: ch1, sc1 into same st as you joined yarn into, sc1 into next st, sc2 into next st, *sc1 into next 2sts, sc2 into next st, rep from * to end, sl st into ch1 at beg of round. (28sts)
Fasten off yarn and join in color of choice to any st from previous round.
Round 4: ch2, dc1 into next 4sts, *ch2, sl st into next st, ch2, dc1 into same st as sl st just worked, dc1 into next 3sts, rep from * to end, ch2, sl st into base of ch2 at beg of round. (7 petals)

Finishing
Fasten off yarn and weave in loose ends. Block if required.
Work each flower as given in different color combinations.

Crocheted Christmas Baubles

SKILL LEVEL

You'll want to make lots of these colorful decorations, perfect for a handmade Christmas gift or to adorn your own boho tree.

YOU WILL NEED

Scraps of DK-weight cotton yarn in 4 assorted colors for each ball
3"-diameter Christmas ball
Size E-4 (3.5mm) hook

Gauge
Gauge is not important in this project

Dimensions
To fit purchased 3"-diameter Christmas ball

To make a ball
(MAKE 2)

Using first color, make magic loop.

Round 1: ch3 (counts as first dc), dc11 into loop, join with a sl st into top of ch3 at beg of round. (12sts) Pull loop tight to close opening. Fasten off yarn and join in color of choice in between any of the sts from previous round.

Round 2: ch3 (counts as first dc), dc1 into same space as ch3, dc2 into each space to end, sl st into top of ch3 at beg of round. (24sts) Fasten off yarn and join in color of choice in between any of the sets of dc2 of previous round.

Round 3: ch3 (counts as first dc), dc2 into same space as ch3, skip next 2sts, *dc3 into next space, rep from * to end, sl st into top of ch3 at beg of round. (36sts) Fasten off yarn and join in color of choice in between any of the sets of dc3 of previous round.

Rounds 4–5: ch3 (counts as first dc), dc2 into same space as ch3, skip next 3sts, *dc3 into next space, rep from * to end, sl st into top of ch3 at beg of round. (36sts) Fasten off yarn and join in color of choice into any of the sts from previous round.

Round 6: ch1, sc1 into same st as ch1, sc1 into each st to end, sl st into ch1 at beg of round. (36sts) Fasten off yarn and weave in loose ends.

Finishing

Once both sections of the ball have been completed, slip both pieces onto your Christmas ball, making sure that the RS are facing out, and sew together, leaving a space for the hanging loop of the ball. Fasten off yarn and weave in loose ends.

Butterfly Pot Holders

⚜ ⚜ ⚜ SKILL LEVEL

Bring a burst of color and a touch of summer to your kitchen with these butterfly-shaped pot holders. Each wing is made up of two disks that are crocheted together.

YOU WILL NEED

Scraps of DK-weight cotton yarn in 7 assorted colors
Size G-6 (4mm) hook

Gauge
Gauge is not important in this project

Dimensions
7¼" high

To make a butterfly mandala

THE DROPS (MAKE 4)

Using color of choice, make a magic loop.

Round 1: ch3 (counts as first st), work [tr1, dc17, tr1, dtr1] into ring, sl st into top of ch3 at beg of round. (21sts)
Fasten off yarn and join in color of choice to dtr of previous round.

Round 2: ch4 (counts as dc1 and ch1), dc1 into same st, dc1 into next 10sts, dc2 into next st, dc1 into each st to end, sl st into third of ch4 at beg of round. (23sts)
Fasten off yarn and join in color of choice to the second stitch of the dc2 at the rounded edge of drop.

Round 3: ch3 (counts as first dc), dc1 into same st, dc1 into next 3sts, dc2 into next 3sts, dc1 into next 3sts, dc2 into next st, work [tr1, ch1, tr1] into chsp of beg ch of round 2, dc2 into next st, dc1 into next 3sts, dc2 into next 3sts, dc1 into next 4sts, dc2 into last st, sl st into top of ch3 at beg of round. (35sts)
Fasten off yarn.

TO JOIN THE DROPS

Using picture as guide, lay out the droplets with all the points toward the center.
Join in color of choice to the st next to sl st of previous round.

Round 4: ch3 (counts as first dc), dc1 into same st, *dc2 into next 2sts, dc1 into next 9sts, dc4tog over next 2sts of first drop and matching 2sts from second drop (drops joined), now work on second drop, dc1 into next 10sts, dc2 into next 3sts, dc1 into next 2sts, dc2 into next 3sts, dc1 into next 4sts, dc4tog over next 2sts of second drop and matching 2sts from third drop (drops joined), dc1 into next 5sts, dc2 into next 3sts, dc1 into next 2sts**, dc2 into next st, rep from *, ending last rep at **, sl st into top of ch3 at beg of round. (121sts)

Fasten off yarn and join in color of choice to the st just before sl st of previous round.

Round 5: ch3 (counts as first st), dc1 into same st, *dc1 into next 6sts, dc2 into next 3sts, dc1 into next 5sts, dc3tog over next 3sts, dc1 into next 5sts, dc2 into next 3sts, dc1 into next 7sts, dc2 into next 2sts, dc1 into next 9sts, dc3tog over next 3sts, dc1 into next 10sts, dc2 into next 2sts, rep from *, ending last rep after first of the last two dc2.

Fasten off yarn and join in color of choice into the first dc st of the third increase (dc2) of the previous round.

Round 6: ch1 (counts as first sc), sc1 into next 5sts, *sc3tog over next 3sts, sc1 into next 14sts, hdc1 into next 3sts, dc2 into next st, work [dc1, tr1] into next st, ch1, work [tr1, dc1] into next st, dc2 into next st, hdc1 into next 3sts, sc1 into next 5sts, sc3tog over next 3sts, sc1 into next 6sts, hdc1 into next 3sts, dc2 into next st, work [dc1, tr1] into next st, ch1, work [tr1, dc1] into next st, dc2 into next st, hdc1 into next 3sts, sc1 into next 13sts, rep from * once more, ending last rep after sc1 has been worked into 7sts.

Fasten off yarn and join in color of choice to the last hdc worked on the previous round.

Round 7: ch1 (counts as first sc), *sc1 into next 12sts, sc3tog over next 3sts, sc1 into next 14sts, hdc1 into next 3sts, dc1 into next 3sts, work [tr2, ch1, tr2] into ch1sp, dc1 into next 3sts, hdc1 into next 3sts, sc1 into next 14sts, hdc1 into next 3sts, dc1 into next 3sts, work [tr2, ch1, tr2] into ch1sp, dc1 into next 3sts, hdc1 into next 3sts **, sc1 into next st, rep from * to **, sl st into ch1 at beg of round. (150sts)

Note: on the next round you will join the center sections of Round 3 using the same color used for Round 3.

Round 8: insert hook into ch1sp of the bottom left droplet, join yarn with sl st, sc1 into same ch1sp, *dc4tog working first two dc into 2sts from same droplet and second two into corresponding sts from next droplet, sc1 into ch1sp of the same droplet as the last two dc worked, rep from * to end, sl st into sc1 at beg of round. Fasten off yarn and weave in loose ends.

Finishing

With WS of pot holder facing you, using same yarn as Round 8, sew the remaining center openings closed. Block if required.

Take time to make sure that your gauge is consistent on each section—otherwise the wings will not be symmetrical.

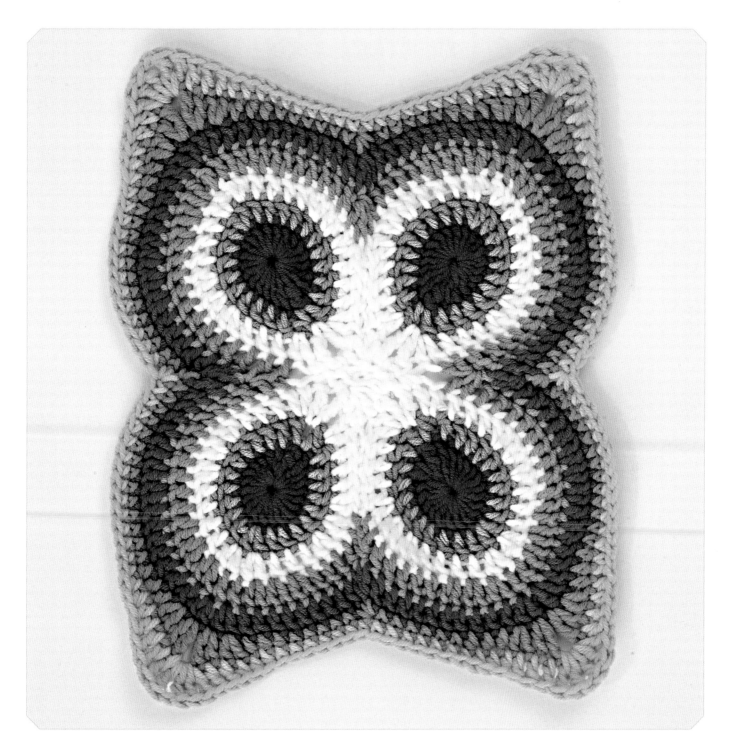

Lace Crochet Coasters

Graduated shades of the same color make a pretty set of coasters with a contrasting trim. Or mix things up and use as many different colors as you like to make as many coasters as you need.

YOU WILL NEED

Scraps of worsted-weight cotton yarn in 6 graduated colors
Scraps of sport-weight cotton yarn in 1 color for edging
Size E-4 (3.5mm) hook
Size B-1 (2.25mm) hook

Gauge
Gauge is not important in this project

Dimensions
Approx 4¾" diameter

To make a coaster (make 6)

Using E-4 hook and color of choice, ch4, join ends with sl st to form ring.

Round 1: ch3 (counts as first dc), dc11 into ring, join with sl st into top of ch3 at beg of round. (12sts)

Round 2: sl st into next sp between dc of previous round, ch3 (counts as first dc), dc1 into same sp, *skip next st, dc2 into next sp, rep from * to end, sl st into top of ch3 at beg of round. (24sts)

Round 3: sl st across next sts and into next sp, ch3 (counts as first st), dc2 into same sp, ch1, *skip 2sts, dc3 into next sp, ch1, rep from * to end, sl st into top of ch3 as beg of round. (36sts)

Round 4: sl st across next 2sts and into next ch1sp, ch3 (counts as first st), dc3 into same sp, ch1, *skip 3sts, dc4 into next ch1sp, ch1, rep from * to end, sl st into top of ch3 at beg of round. (48sts)

Round 5: ch1 (counts as first sc), sc1 into each st and ch1sp to end, sl st into ch1 at beg of round. (60sts) Fasten off yarn.

Using B-1 hook and edging yarn, join yarn to any st of previous round.

Round 6: ch1, sc1 into first st, ch2, hdc1 into base of sc just worked, skip next st, *work [sc1, ch2, hdc1] into base of sc just worked, skip next st, rep from *, ending last rep with sl st into ch1 at beg of round.

Finishing

Fasten off yarn and weave in loose ends. Block if required.
Make five more in different colors.

Breakfast Cozy Set

✦ **SKILL LEVEL**

Brighten up the breakfast table with a set of granny-square cozies for your French press and coffee mugs; maybe even add a set of coordinating coasters.

YOU WILL NEED

Scraps of worsted-weight cotton yarn in 5 assorted colors
2 buttons ¾" diameter for French press
1 button ¾" diameter for mug cozy
Size G-6 (4mm) hook

Gauge
Gauge is not important in this project

Dimensions
French press cozy 8½" high
Coaster 4" square
Mug cozy 8½" x 4"

To make the French press cozy

GRANNY SQUARE (MAKE 2)

Using color of choice, ch5, join ends with sl st to form ring.

Round 1: ch3 (counts as first dc), dc2 into ring, *ch3, dc3 into ring, rep from * twice more, ch3, sl st into top of ch3 at beg of round. (4 sets of dc3)

Fasten off yarn and join new color into any of the ch3sp.

Round 2: ch3 (counts as first dc), work [dc2, ch3, dc3] into same ch3sp, *ch1, skip next 3sts, work [dc3, ch3, dc3] into next ch3sp, rep from * twice more, ch1, sl st into top of ch3 at beg of round. (8 sets of dc3)

Fasten off yarn and join new color into any of the ch3sp.

Round 3: ch3 (counts as first dc), work [dc2, ch3, dc3] into same ch3sp, *ch1, skip next 3sts, dc3 in ch1sp, ch1**, work [dc3, ch3, dc3] into next ch3sp, rep from * 3 more times, ending last rep at **, sl st into top of ch3 at beg of round. (12 sets of dc3)

Fasten off yarn and join new color into any of the ch3sp.

Round 4: ch3 (counts as first dc), work [dc2, ch3, dc3] into same ch3sp, *[ch1, skip next 3sts, dc3 into ch1sp, ch1] twice**, work [dc3, ch3, dc3] into next ch3sp, rep from * 3 more times, ending last rep at **, sl st into top of ch3 at beg of round. (16 sets of dc3)

Fasten off yarn and join new color into any of the ch3sp.

Round 5: ch3 (counts as first dc), work [dc2, ch3, dc3] into same ch3sp, *[ch1, skip next 3sts, dc3 into ch1sp, ch1] 3 times**, work [dc3, ch3, dc3] into next ch3sp, rep from * 3 more times, ending last rep at **, sl st into top of ch3 at beg of round. (20 sets of dc3)

Weave in loose ends, then sew the two squares together using same color as the outer edge along one side.

Finishing

With RS facing you and using color of choice, join yarn to first st after top right ch2sp edge as follows.

Round 1: ch1 (counts as first sc), sc1 into each st, ch1sp and seam to next corner, work [sc3 into ch3sp, sc1 into each st and ch1sp to next corner] twice, sc3 into next ch3sp, ch11 (button loop made), sc1 into next 17sts, ch11, sc1 into next st, sc3 into last ch3sp, join with sl st into ch1 at beg of round.

Fasten yarn and weave in loose ends. Sew buttons onto RS at the opposite side from button loops.

To make the coaster

GRANNY SQUARE (MAKE 1)

Work Rounds 1–4 as given for French press cozy. Fasten off yarn and weave in loose ends.

Using color of choice, join yarn to any stitch from previous round and work edge as follows.

Round 5: ch1 (counts as first sc), sc1 into each st and ch1sp to first corner, *work sc3 into ch3sp, sc1 into each st and ch1sp to next corner, rep from * twice more, sc3 into last ch3sp, sc1 into each st to end, sl st into ch1 at beg of round. Fasten off yarn. Weave in loose ends.

To make the mug cozy

GRANNY SQUARE (MAKE 2)

Work Rounds 1–3 as given for French press cozy. Fasten off yarn. Using color of choice, join yarn to any stitch from previous round and work edge as follows.

Round 4: ch1 (counts as first sc), sc1 into each st, ch1sp and seam to first corner, *work sc3 into ch3sp, sc1 into each st and ch1sp to next corner, rep from * twice more, sc3 into last ch3sp, sc1 into each st to end, sl st into ch1 at beg of round. Weave in loose ends. Sew the two squares together using same color as the outer edge along one side.

Finishing

Make strap as follows.

With RS facing and granny squares lying vertically, join color of choice to first st after sc3 into ch3sp at the top right-hand corner.

Row 1: ch1, sc1 into same st, sc1 into next 8sts, turn. (9sts)

Rows 2–6: ch1, sc1 into each st to end, turn.

Wrap cozy around mug to see whether you need any extra rows and add here if required.

Row 7: ch1, sc1 into next 3sts, ch3, skip next 3sts, sc1 into each st to end. Fasten off yarn.

Round 1: ch1 (counts as first sc), *sc1 into each st to center of sc3 from round 4 of the motif, sc2 into next st, rep from * 3 more times, work sc1 into each st along edge and across the top of the strap to ch3sp, sc3 into ch3sp, sc1 into each st to end of round, sl st into ch1 at beg of round.

Fasten off yarn and weave in loose ends. Sew button onto opposite edge from strap.

Crochet
FASHION

Boho crochet fashion accessories are fun to wear and a great way to add color to your wardrobe. Keep the look subdued with a simple hairband or necklace, or make a statement with a shawl or scarf.

Drops of Color Headband

The shapes that make up this cascading drops headband are
super easy to make and highly addictive.

YOU WILL NEED

Scraps of Aran-weight cotton yarn in
8 assorted colors
Headband
Hot-glue gun
Size H-8 (5mm) hook, or you can use a hook
one size smaller for sturdier drops

Gauge
Gauge is not important in this project

Dimensions
A drop measures 1½" x 1¼"

To make the headband

THE DROPS (MAKE 8)
Using color of choice, make
magic loop.
Round 1: ch3 (counts as first dc),
work [dc1, sc17, dc1, tr1, dtr1] into
loop, join with sl st into top of ch3 at
beg of round. (22sts)
Pull loop tight and weave in
loose ends.
Make a further 7 drops using each
of the colors.

Finishing
Using picture as guide, pull each
drop into correct shape and block
if required.

Decorating the headband
Using picture as guide, place each
of the drops at a slight angle on the
headband one at a time, glue into
position, and leave to dry before
adding the next drop.

Floral Bobby Pins

❀ ❀ SKILL LEVEL

Pretty flowers turn plain bobby pins into a fun hair accessory for girls of all ages.
Use scraps of yarn to make a bouquet of them so that you have one to match every outfit.

YOU WILL NEED

Scraps of sport-weight cotton yarn in colors
of choice
Pearl beads
Bobby pins
Hot-glue gun
Size C-2 (2.75mm) hook

Gauge

Gauge is not important in this project

Dimensions

A flower measures approx 1¾" in diameter

To make a flower

Using color of choice, ch2.
Round 1: sc10 into 2nd ch from
hook, sl st into first of ch2 at beg
of round.
Round 2: ch2, dc1 into first 2sts,
ch2, sl st into same st as last dc
worked, *ch2, dc1 into next 2sts,
ch2, sl st into same st as last dc
worked, rep from * to end. (5 petals)
Round 3: working behind Round
2, sl st into stitch between petals
(hook 2 loops to create a stable base
to work from), *ch4, sl st in stitch
between next petal, rep from * 4
times, ch4 sl st into first sl st to
close. (5ch4loops)

Round 4: sl st into first ch4sp, ch2,
work [dc4, ch2] into same ch4sp,
*ch2, work [dc4, ch2] into next
ch4sp, rep from * to end. (5 petals)
Fasten off yarn and weave in
loose ends.

Finishing

Glue the pearl bead to the center
of the flower and leave to dry. Glue
the bobby pin to the back of crochet
flower and leave to dry.

Rainbow Wrist Cuffs

Make these gloves and your hands will thank you—they're
colorful, warm, and stylish too.

YOU WILL NEED

Scraps of sport-weight wool blend yarn in
the following colors

MC	aqua
CCa	red
CCb	pink
CCc	light blue
CCd	teal
CCe	gold
CCf	lilac
CCg	medium blue
CCh	light green

14 buttons, ¼" diameter
Size E-4 (3.5mm) hook

Gauge
20 stitches by 11 rows over 4" square
using dc

Dimensions
Pattern is written to fit woman's medium-
sized hand.
To make larger, add a multiple of 3 to the
chain at the beginning of the pattern.
To make smaller, reduce by a multiple of 3
at the beginning of the pattern.

To make the mitts

LEFT MITT

Using CCa, ch38.
Row 1: hdc1 into 3rd ch from
hook, hdc1 into each ch to end,
turn. (36sts)
Fasten off CCa and join in CCb.
Row 2: ch3, dc1 into each st to
end, turn.
Work the next 13 rows as Row 2,
changing color for each row to create
stripe as follows.
Row 3: CCc.
Row 4: CCd.
Row 5: CCe.
Row 6: CCf.
Row 7: CCg.
Row 8: CCb.
Row 9: MC.
Row 10: CCh.
Row 11: CCa.
Row 12: CCd.
Row 13: CCc.
Row 14: CCe.
Row 15: CCb.

Work the next section of the mitt
as rounds.
Fasten off CCb and join in CCf.
Round 16: ch3, dc1 into each st
to end, sl st into top of ch3 at beg
of round.
Work the next two rounds as Round
16, changing color for each round to
create stripe as follows.
Round 17: CCg.
Round 18: CCh.
Fasten off CCh and join in CCa.
Round 19: ch2, hdc1 into each st
to end, sl st into top of ch2 at beg
of round.
Fasten off CCa and join in MC.

TOP EDGING

Round 20: ch1, sc1 into each st to
end, sl st into ch1 at beg of round.
Do not fasten off yarn.
Work next round working sl sts into
back loops only.

Round 21: *ch3, sl st into same st (picot made), sl st into next 3sts, rep from * to end.
Fasten off yarn.

Button band

Lay mitt out so the rounds are on the left-hand side and the fold is to the bottom.
With RS facing you, join MC to the top right-hand corner and work button band as follows.
Row 1: ch3 (counts as first st), work dc2 into each stripe until 23sts have been worked.
Fasten off yarn.

Buttonhole band

With RS facing you and using MC, work buttonhole band on opposite side from button band just worked. Join yarn to twelfth stripe from the left.
Row 1: ch1, sc1 into same sp, sc2 into each stripe to end, turn. (23sts)
Row 2: ch1, sc1 into first st, sc1 into next st, *ch2, skip 1st, sc1 into each of next 2sts, rep from * to end, turn. (7 buttonholes)
Row 3: skip 1st, sl st into next st, *sc3 into ch2sp, sl st into next 2sts, rep from * 5 more times, sc3 into ch2sp, skip 1st, sl st in last st in row.
Fasten off yarn and weave in loose ends.

Thumb hole

With RS facing, start work where the button band finished, into the thirteenth stripe.
Join MC into thirteenth stripe.
Round 1: ch1, sc2 into same place as ch1 just worked, continue working sc2 into each stripe up to where the rounds begin, next work back down the stripes until you have 16sts, skip the buttonhole band sts, working the first st firmly, work sc2 into the end of button band, sl st into first sc at beg of round. (18sts)
Round 2: ch1, sc1 into each st to end, sl st into ch1 at beg of round.
Fasten off yarn.

Right mitt

Work as given for left mitt until all 21 rows/rounds of mitt and top edging have been completed.

Buttonhole band

Lay mitt out so the rounds are on the left-hand side and the fold is to the bottom.
Join MC to top right-hand corner and work buttonhole band as given for left mitt.

Button band

With RS facing you, join MC to twelfth stripe from left and work button band on opposite side from buttonhole band as for left mitt.

Thumb hole

Work to match left mitt.

Finishing

Weave in loose ends and sew buttons onto button bands to match up with buttonholes.

Use scraps of yarn to make these colorful, striped wrist cuffs and dig into your jar of buttons to add a mismatched row of buttons.

Slouch Hat

SKILL LEVEL

This cozy hat is perfect for crisp fall days. The popcorn stitch adds texture and helps to showcase the soft, hand-dyed yarn.

YOU WILL NEED

Bulky-weight baby alpaca yarn (approx 3.5 oz/100 g; 109 yds/100 m)
MC   1 ball in variegated orange/pink/ orchid
Size J-10 (6mm) hook

Gauge
4 popcorns to 4"

Dimensions
To fit a head 22" in circumference

Special stitches
Popcorn stitch (dc4pop): work dc4 into the same stitch, drop loop from hook, insert hook from front to back through the top of the first dc and back into dropped loop, then pull it through the st to close
Popcorn stitch (dc3pop): work dc3 into the same stitch, drop loop from hook, insert hook from front to back through the top of the first dc and back into dropped loop, then pull it through the st to close

To make the hat

Using MC, make magic loop.

Round 1: ch3 (counts as first dc), work dc11 into ring, join with sl st into top of ch3 at beg of round. (12sts)

Round 2: ch3 (counts as first dc), dc1 into same place as base of ch3 just worked, dc2 into each st to end, sl st into ch3 at beg of round. (24sts)

Round 3: ch3 (counts as first dc), *dc2 into next st, dc1 into next st, rep from * to last st, dc2 into last st, sl st into top of ch3 at beg of round.

Round 4: ch3 (counts as first dc), work dc3pop into base of ch3, ch2, skip 1st, *dc4pop into next st, ch2, skip 1st, rep from * to end, sl st into top of first popcorn. (18 popcorns)

Round 5: sl st into first ch2sp, ch3 (counts as first dc), dc3 into same ch2sp, *skip popcorn, dc4 into next ch2sp, rep from * to end, sl st into top of ch3 at beg of round. (72sts)

Round 6: ch3 (counts as first dc), dc1 into next 2sts, dc2 into next st, *dc1 into next 3sts, dc2 into next st, rep from * to end, sl st into top of ch3 at beg of round. (90sts)

Round 7: ch3 (counts as first dc), work dc3pop into base of ch3, ch2, *skip 2sts, dc4pop into next st, rep from * to end, sl st into top of first popcorn. (30 popcorns)

Round 8: sl st into first ch2sp, ch3 (counts as first dc), dc1 into same ch2sp, *skip popcorn, dc2 into next ch2sp, rep from * to end, sl st into top of ch3 at beg of round. (60sts)

Round 9: ch3 (counts as first dc), dc1 into each st to end.

Round 10: as Round 7. (20 popcorns)

Round 11: sl st into first ch2sp, ch3 (counts as first dc), dc2 into same ch2sp, *skip popcorn, dc3 into next ch2sp, rep from * to end, sl st into top of ch3 at beg of round. (60sts)

Round 12: as Round 9.

Round 13: as Round 7.
(20 popcorns)
Round 14: as Round 8. (40sts)
Round 15: as Round 9.
Round 16: ch1 (counts as first sc),
sc2 into next st, *sc1 into next st,
sc2 into next st, rep from * to end,
sl st into ch1 at beg of round. (60sts)
Round 17: ch1 (counts as first sc),
sc1 into each st to end, sl st into ch1
at beg of round.
Repeat Round 17 twice more.

Finishing
Fasten off yarn and weave in
loose ends.

Soft alpaca yarn makes this hat a pleasure to wear– and it will garner compliments whenever you wear it.

Dancing Hearts Wrap

Perfect for cool summer evenings and early fall mornings,
this heart-shaped wrap will keep the chill away.

YOU WILL NEED

Sport-weight acrylic yarn
(approx 3.5 oz/100 g; 350 yds/311 m)
MC   1 ball in white
CCa   1 ball in light green
CCb   1 ball in medium green
CCc   1 ball in dark pink
CCd   1 ball in light pink
Size J-10 (6mm) hook

Gauge

Gauge is not important for this project but
you will find it easier to use a hook one size
larger than required by the yarn

Dimensions

60" x 32"
From edge to edge this heart-shaped wrap is
60" long. The heart shape is 32" deep

Special stitches

Popcorn stitch (tr3pop): work
tr3 in indicated st, drop loop from
hook, insert hook from front to back
through the top of the first tr of the
group, use hook to pull the dropped
loop through the st to close. The
first popcorn stitch of the round is
worked with a ch4 as the first treble.

To make the wrap

Using CCa, make magic loop.
Round 1: ch4 (counts as first tr),
tr2pop into loop (first popcorn
made), ch2, *tr3pop into loop, ch2,
rep from * 10 more times, sl st into
top of first popcorn. (12 popcorns)
Pull loop tight to close.
Round 2: ch7 (counts as tr1 and
ch3), *tr1 into next ch2sp, ch3,
rep from * 10 more times, sl st into
fourth of ch7 at beg of round.
(12 ch3sp)
Fasten off MC and join in CCc into
any ch3sp.

Round 3: ch2 (counts as first st),
work [hdc2, dc1, ch1, dc1, hdc3]
into same ch3sp, *skip next st, work
[hdc3, dc1, ch1, dc1, hdc3] into next
ch3sp, rep from * 10 more times,
sl st into top of ch2 at beg of round.
Round 4: ch1 (counts as first st),
*skip next 3sts, work [dc4, ch2, dc4]
into next ch1sp, skip next 3sts**,
sc1 in between next 2sts, rep from *
11 more times, ending last rep at **,
sl st into ch1 at beg of round.
Fasten off and weave in loose ends.
Make a further 15 motifs as above,
finishing after Round 4, and a
further 18 motifs using CCb
for Rounds 1–2 and CCd for
Rounds 3–4.

Assembling the heart shape

Lay the motifs out in a heart shape
before joining them. Lay 9 motifs
in a shallow V shape (this will be
the bottom edge). Alternate colors
between light and dark motifs, so

the edge motifs and center motif are light pink. Place a dark motif directly above the center motif, and lay another 4 motifs each side, alternating colors. Place a light motif above the second-row center motif, and lay another 4 motifs each side, alternating colors. For the final V, place the center motif above the center motif of the previous row and place 3 motifs each side to complete the heart shape.

Finishing

For each new motif, join MC to any sc on Round 4.

Round 5 (first motif): sc1 into same st, *ch4, skip 4 sts, work into next ch2sp [sc1, ch1, sc1], ch4, skip 4 sts**, sc1 into next sc, rep from *, ending last rep at **, sl st into sc1 at beg of round.

Fasten off.

The repeated flower motifs are joined together using single crochet and slip stitches, which complement the lacy texture of the shawl.

Round 5 (each remaining motif): sc1 into same st, *ch4, skip 4 sts, work into next ch2sp either a joining edging-point [sc1, ch1, join with sl st into ch1sp of edged motif, sc1] or a free edging-point [sc1, ch1, sc1], ch4, skip 4 sts**, sc1 into next sc, rep from *, ending last rep at **,

joining each motif into two of the ch2sp of the adjoining motif before joining into two of the ch2sp of the next adjacent edged motif (if there is one), to end the round, sl st into sc1 at beg of round.

Fasten off and weave in loose ends. Block wrap if required.

Wildflowers Scarf

Wrap yourself in a colorful garland of wildflowers. Wear the design long and skinny, layered like a cowl, or around your waist as a decorative belt.

YOU WILL NEED

Scraps of DK-weight cotton or wool yarn in assorted colors
Size G-6 (4mm) hook

Gauge
Gauge is not important in this project

Dimensions
A flower measures approx 4½" wide

To make the scarf

FIRST FLOWER MOTIF

Using color of choice, ch6, join ends tog with sl st to form ring.

Round 1: ch3 (counts as first dc), dc23 into ring, sl st into top of ch3 at beg of round. (24sts)
Fasten off yarn and join color of choice into any st.

Round 2: ch6 (counts as sc1 and ch5), *skip 1st, sc1, ch3, skip 1st, sc1, ch5, rep from * 4 more times, skip 1st, sc1, ch3, sl st into first of ch6 at beg of round. (12 spaces)

Round 3: ch3 (counts as first dc), work [dc3, ch3, dc4] into ch5sp, *sc1 into next ch3sp, work [dc4, ch3, dc4] into next ch5sp, rep from * 4 more times, sc1 into last ch3sp, sl st into top of ch3 at beg of round. (6 petals)
Fasten off yarn and weave in loose ends.

SECOND FLOWER MOTIF

Work Rounds 1–2 as given for first flower using colors of choice.
Join flowers together on Round 3 by working a sl st into matching ch3sp of top two petals, making sure the WS are together when joining as follows.

Round 3: ch3 (counts as first dc), work [dc3, ch1, sl st into corresponding ch3sp of first flower, ch1, dc4] into first ch5sp, sc1 into next ch3sp, work [dc4, sl st into corresponding ch3sp of first flower, ch1, dc4] into next ch5sp, *sc1 into next ch3sp, work [dc4, ch3, dc4] into next ch5sp, rep from * 3 more times, sc1 into last ch3sp, sl st into top of ch3 at beg of round.
Keep working motifs as given for second flower until scarf is required length.

Finishing
Weave in loose ends and block if required.

Ombré String Cowl

This unusual cowl is perfect for crisp early fall mornings—it adds just the right layer of warmth while you wait for the sun to work its magic.

YOU WILL NEED

Scraps of worsted-weight acrylic yarn

MC	berry
CCa	magenta
CCb	dark rose
CCc	light rose
CCd	pink

Size I-9 (5.5mm) hook

Gauge

Gauge is not important in this project

Dimensions

7" wide and 25" circumference

Special stitches

Back loop only (blo): the back loop of a chain refers to the back loop of the "V" on the front of the chain. Put your hook through this loop when stitching into the ch.

To make the cowl

Using MC, ch90, join ends with sl st to form ring.

Round 1: ch1, sc1 into blo of each ch to end, join with sl st into ch1 at beg of round. (90sts)

Fasten off MC and join in CCa.

Round 2: sl st into blo of each st to end, sl st into first sl st at beg of round.

Round 3: ch1, sc1 into blo of same place as join, ch29, skip next 29sts, *sc1 into next st on Round 1, ch29, skip next 29sts, rep from * once more, join with sl st into ch1 at beg of round.

Round 4: ch1, sc1 into blo of each st and ch to end, sl st into ch1 at beg of round.

Break off yarn and join in CCb. The last three rounds form pattern; repeat Rounds 2–4 as follows.

Rounds 5–7: CCb.
Rounds 8–10: CCc.
Rounds 11–13: CCd.
Rounds 14–16: CCc.
Rounds 17–19: CCb.
Rounds 20–22: CCa.
Rounds 23–25: MC.
Round 26: as Round 2.

Finishing

Fasten off yarn and weave in loose ends.

Blossom Necklace

Adorn yourself with a necklace of colorful flowers. This delightful lariat-style necklace wraps and drapes daintily so why not crochet in all your favorite colors, from bold brights to soft pastels.

YOU WILL NEED

Scraps of sock, fingering, or sport-weight yarn—any smooth yarn with good stitch definition will work well in this project. You could also experiment with novelty yarns
Size D-3 (3.25 mm) hook

Gauge
Gauge is not important in this project

Dimensions
A flower measures approx 1½" x 1½"

To make the scarf

FLOWER CENTER
Using color of choice, make magic loop.
Round 1: ch2 (counts as first hdc), work hdc17 into ring, sl st into top of ch2 at beg of round. (18hdc)
Fasten off yarn.

PETALS
Using color of choice, join into any stitch of the flower center with a sl st.
Round 1: ch3 (counts as first dc), dc3 into the same st, sc1 into next 2sts, *dc4 into next st, sc1 into next 2sts, rep from * to end, sl st into top of ch3 at beg of round.
Fasten off yarn.
Make as many flowers as you wish in the colors of your choice.

STEM
With WS of flower facing, sl st into back loop of any of the sc petal stitches, ch4, skip hdc, and sl st into base of stitch straight across from first sl st, ch10, then attach next flower in exactly the same way. Continue joining the flowers together until they have all been attached or the flower chain is the required length. Once you have attached the final flower work a further ch3.

Finishing
Fasten off yarn and weave in loose ends.

Granny-Square Clutch Purse

Join pretty granny squares to make a clutch purse big enough to hold everything you need for a night out. Alternatively, brighten your desk using this colorful clutch as a pencil case.

YOU WILL NEED

Sport-weight cotton yarn
(approx 1.76 oz/50 g; 132 yds/121 m)
MC   1 ball in white
Scraps of yarn in 8 assorted colors
4 buttons, ¾" diameter
Size C-2 (2.75mm) hook

Gauge
A square measures 2" x 2"

Dimensions
4¼" x 7¾"

To make the clutch purse

GRANNY SQUARE (MAKE 16)
Using color of choice, ch4 (counts as ch1 and dc1).
Round 1: dc1 into 4th ch from hook, ch1, *dc2 into same ch as first st, ch1, rep from * 5 more times, sl st into top of initial ch4. (8 petals)
Sl st into first dc of Round 1 and break off yarn. Join color of choice into first ch1sp.
Round 2: ch3 (counts as first dc), dc2 into same ch1sp, *skip next 2sts, work [dc3, ch2, dc3] into next ch1sp**, skip 2sts, dc3 into next ch1sp, rep from * 3 more times, ending last rep at **, sl st into top of ch3 at beg of round.
Fasten off yarn and join MC into first dc of dc3 on any side.
Round 3: ch1, sc1 into next 5sts, *work [sc1, ch1, sc1] into next ch2sp, sc1 into next 9sts, rep from * twice more, work [sc1, ch1, sc1] into last ch2sp, sc1 into last 3sts, sl st into ch1 at beg of round.
Weave in loose ends.

Finishing

Sew the squares together as follows. Place first two squares with RS together, then using MC, work whipstitch through the back loops only. Repeat this process until you have two sets of 2 x 4 squares. With RS facing you and using MC, join yarn to first st just after the corner.
Round 1: ch1, *sc1 into each st to corner, work [sc1, ch1, sc1] into corner (corner made), rep from * to end, sl st into ch1 at beg of round. Repeat Round 1 once more.
Fasten off yarn.
Place panels with RS together, then sew together using same method as squares. Work around three edges only, leaving top open.
Weave in loose ends and turn clutch RS out.

Using picture as guide, attach a button to the center top of each square just below the opening.
Turn clutch over so the opposite side from the button panel is facing.
Using MC, join yarn to center top of square, making sure you match position of each button, ch6, skip 1st and sl st into next st.
Fasten off yarn and weave in loose ends.
Repeat this for remaining buttons.

Cell Phone and Tablet Covers

Use up all your odds and ends of yarn and give your phone and tablet
a unique and colorful protective cover.

YOU WILL NEED

Scraps of DK-weight acrylic/nylon blend yarn

CCa	1 ball in yellow
CCb	1 ball in light green
CCc	1 ball in red
CCd	1 ball in purple
CCe	1 ball in orange
CCf	1 ball in pink
CCg	1 ball in blue

3 buttons ¾" diameter for phone cover

4 buttons 1½" diameter for tablet cover

Size G-6 (4 mm) hook

Size H-8 (5 mm) hook

Gauge

Not important but check to make sure panel
will fit cell phone or tablet snugly

Dimensions

Cell phone cover: 6" x 3½"

Tablet cover: 9½" x 7"

To make the cell phone cover

PANEL (MAKE 2)

Using H-8 hook and CCa, ch23.
Change to G-6 hook.

Row 1: sc1 into 2nd ch from hook,
sc1 into each ch to end, turn. (22sts)

Row 2: ch1 (counts as first st), sc1
into each st and tch to end. (22sts)

Fasten off CCa and join in CCb.
Work each row as Row 2 in the
following stripe sequence:

Rows 3 and 4: CCb.

Rows 5 and 6: CCc.

Rows 7 and 8: CCd.

Rows 9 and 10: CCe.

Rows 11 and 12: CCf.

Fasten off yarn and weave in
loose ends.

Block front and back panels to
correct size.

Finishing

With WS together, join front and
back panels as follows using yarn
CCg and G-6 hook.

Insert hook at the top right-hand
corner of both front and back panels,
yo and draw through, work sl st to
secure, ch1, sc1 into same place as
you joined the yarn, *work sc1 into
each stitch, matching up the front
and back panels until you reach
first corner, work sc3 into corner
(first corner made), rep from * until
second corner made, then continue
working back up to the top opening.
Do not fasten off yarn.

Work top opening in rounds
as follows.

Round 1: ch1, work sc1 into each
stitch around the opening, sl st into
ch1 at beg of round.

Fasten off CCg and join in CCc.

Next round: ch1, sc1 into each st
from joining of the panels, working
sc3 into each corner, then work as
Round 1 of top opening.

Fasten off yarn and weave in
loose ends.

To make the tablet cover

PANEL (MAKE 2)

Using H-8 hook and CCa, ch38.
Change to G-6 hook.

Row 1: sc1 into 2nd ch from hook, sc1 into each ch to end, turn. (38sts)

Row 2: ch1 (counts as first sc), sc1 into each st and tch to end, turn.

The last row forms pattern; repeat Row 2 twice more.

Work each row as Row 2 in the following stripe sequence:

Rows 5–8: CCb.

Rows 9–12: CCc.

Rows 13–16: CCd.

Rows 17–20: CCe.

Rows 21–24: CCf.

Rows 25–28: CCg.

Rows 29–32: CCa.

Rows 33–36: CCb.

Fasten off yarn and weave in loose ends.

Block front and back panels to correct size.

Finishing

With WS together, join front and back panels together as follows using CCc and G-6 hook.

Insert hook at the top right-hand corner of both front and back panels, yo and draw through, work sl st to secure, ch1, sc1 into same place as you joined the yarn, *work sc1 into each stitch, matching up the front and back panels, until you reach first corner, work sc3 into corner (first corner made), repeat from * until second corner made, then continue working back up to the top opening. Do not fasten off yarn.

Work top opening in rounds as follows.

Round 1: ch1, work sc1 into each stitch around the opening, sl st into ch1 at beg of round.

Fasten off CCc and join in CCd.

Round 2: as Round 1.

Round 2 forms repeat; repeat in the following stripe sequence.

Round 3: CCe.

Round 4: CCf.

Round 5: CCg.

Fasten off yarn and weave in loose ends.

To make the loop

Using G-6 hook and CCb, and leaving long tail, ch24, join ends with sl st form loop.

Round 1: ch1, sc24 into loop, sl st into ch1 at beg of round.

Fasten off yarn, leaving long tail.

Pin loop to inside center back of case just below the start of the top opening.

Stitch into position using long tails.

Sew button to center front panel to match loop, then add three more buttons for decoration if desired.

This design features
vertical stripes rather
than the usual
horizontal ones.
Summery seaside
colors add to the fun.

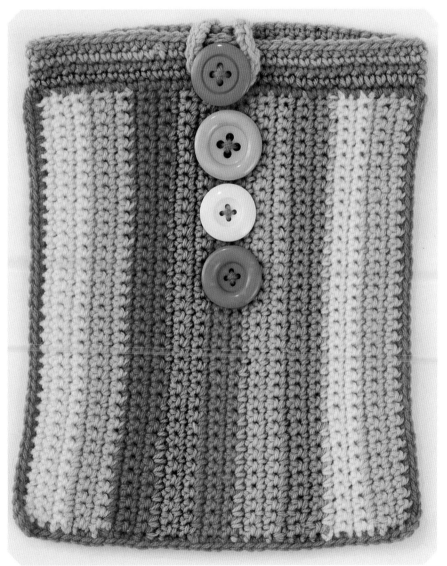

Star Backpack

Youngsters—and the young at heart—will enjoy filling this spacious bag with their belongings. Keep an eye on your work so that the stitches are close together and there are no gaps in the fabric.

YOU WILL NEED

Scraps of sport-weight cotton yarn in
14 assorted colors
Size C-2 (2.75 mm) hook for bag and stars
Size G-6 (4 mm) hook for bag ties
Fiberfill for stuffing stars

Gauge
Gauge is not important in this project

Dimensions
16½" high

To make the bag

BASE (MAKE 1)
Using C-2 hook and color of choice, ch4, join ends with sl st to form ring.

Round 1: ch3 (counts as first dc), dc10 into ring, sl st into top of ch3 at beg of round. (11sts)

Round 2: ch3 (counts as first dc), dc1 into same st, dc2 into each st to end, sl st into top of ch3 at beg of round. (22sts)

Round 3: ch3 (counts as first dc), dc1 into same st, dc1 into next st, *dc2 into next st, dc1 into next st, rep from * to end, sl st into top of ch3 at beg of round. (33sts)

Round 4: ch3 (counts as first dc), dc1 into same st, dc1 into next 2sts, *dc2 into next st, dc1 into next 2sts, rep from * to end, sl st into top of ch3 at beg of round. (44sts)

Round 5: ch3 (counts as first dc), dc1 into same st, dc1 into next 3sts, *dc2 into next st, dc1 into next 3sts, rep from * to end, sl st into top of ch3 at beg of round. (55sts)

Round 6: ch3 (counts as first dc), dc1 into same st, dc1 into next 4sts, *dc2 into next st, dc1 into next 4sts, rep from * to end, sl st into top of ch3 at beg of round. (66sts)

Fasten off yarn and join in color of choice.

Keep working as set, adding 1st every round in between increases until 231sts.

To make the bag smaller, stop increasing when the finished number of stitches is divisible by 3.

To make the bag bigger, continue increasing as set, finishing when the number of stitches is divisible by 3.

BODY (MAKE 1)
Make body of bag as follows, changing colors at the end of each round to create the stripe pattern.

Round 1: ch4 (counts as dc1 and ch1), dc1 into same st, *skip 2sts, work [dc1, ch1, dc1] into next st, rep from * to end, sl st into 3rd ch of ch4 at beg of round.
Sl st into ch1sp, fasten off yarn, and join in color of choice.
Round 2: ch4 (counts as dc1 and ch1), dc1 into ch1sp, *skip 2sts, work [dc1, ch1, dc1] into next ch1sp, rep from * to end, sl st into 3rd ch of ch4 at beg of round.
Repeat Round 2 until 28 rounds have been worked or bag is required length.
Fasten off yarn and weave in loose ends.

TOP FLAP
Using C-2 hook and color of choice, ch42.
Row 1: dc1 into 4th ch from hook, dc1 into each ch to end, turn. (39sts + 1tch)

Row 2: ch3 (counts as first dc), dc1 into each st and tch, turn. (40sts)
Fasten off yarn and join in color of choice.
Repeat Row 2 until nine rows have been worked, changing color every two rows to form stripe.
Row 10: ch3 (counts as first dc), dc2tog over next 2sts, dc1 into each st until 1st remains, skip the last st, turn. (38sts)
Repeat Row 10 until 22sts, keeping stripe correct.
Fasten off yarn and join in color of choice.
Work edging around top flap as follows.
Round 1: ch1, sc2 around each st up to top, sc1 along straight edge, sc2 around each st down the side to bottom section, sc1 along to beg of round, sl st into ch1 at beg of round.
Fasten off yarn and join in color of choice.
Round 2: as Round 1.
Fasten off yarn.
Attach top flap to bag, pinning into position, and then sew into place.

Bag handles (make 2)

Using C-2 hook and color of choice, ch13.
Row 1: dc1 into 4th ch from hook, dc1 into each ch to end, turn. (11sts)
Row 2: ch3, dc1 into each st to end, turn.
Repeat last row until approx 102 rows have been worked or until handle is required length.
Pin and stitch both handles into position at top and bottom of the bag.
Weave in loose ends.

Bag ties

Using G-6 hook and six strands of yarn held together, work chain until required length.
Fasten off yarn.
Weave chain through top row of Vs of bag.

Stars (make 2)

This design is worked in a spiral.
Do not close rounds with a sl st; place a marker to help you identify where the end of the round is.
Using C-2 hook and color of choice, ch2.
Round 1: sc5 into 2nd ch from hook. (5sts)
Round 2: sc2 into each st to end. (10sts)
Round 3: *sc1 into next st, sc2 into next st, rep from * to end. (15sts)
Round 4: *sc1 into next 2sts, sc2 into next st, rep from * to end. (20sts)

Work star points as follows in rows.
Row 1: sc1 into next 4sts, turn. (4sts)
Row 2: ch1, sc1 into each st to end, turn. (4sts)
Row 3: ch1, skip next st, sc1 into each st to end, turn. (3sts)
Repeat Row 3.
Fasten off yarn.
Rejoin yarn to next st after the base of first point on main spiral section and repeat rows.
On the last point, do not fasten off yarn. Work edge as follows.
Work *sc4 down point, sl st in between points, sc4 up next point, sc1 into top of point, rep from * until all five points have been worked.
Fasten off yarn and weave in loose ends. Block if required.

Finishing

Place stars with WS together and sew around the outer edge, inserting stuffing as you go. Use a pencil or similar to make sure the stuffing fills the point.
Sew star to the bag ties.
Repeat pattern for second star using a different color.

The Weekender Bag

Destined to become your favorite bag, this tote is lots of fun to make and perfect
for weekend adventures—or for holding your yarn stash.

Large bag

YOU WILL NEED

Worsted-weight acrylic yarn (approx
3.5 oz/100 g; 170 yds/156 m)
MC   2 balls in white
CCa   1 ball in rust
CCb   1 ball in terra cotta
23" zipper for large bag
2 metal circle rings, 1½" diameter, for
attaching handle
44"-long strap with latch hooks on each end
Size F-5 (3.75mm) hook for base
Size G-6 (4mm) hook for bag

Gauge

Using F-5 hook, approx 20 stitches by 18
rows over 4" square using pattern
Using G-6 hook, approx 16 stitches by 16
rows over 4" square using pattern

Dimensions

Approx 6" x 16" at bottom, 15" tall, 23"
across the top

Small bag

YOU WILL NEED

Worsted-weight acrylic yarn (approx
3.5 oz/100 g; 170 yds/156 m)
MC   2 balls in white
CCa   1 ball in honey
CCb   1 ball in mustard
18" zipper for small bag
2 metal circle rings, 1½" diameter, for
attaching handle
44"-long strap with latch hooks on each end
Size F-5 (3.75mm) hook for base
Size G-6 (4mm) hook for bag

Gauge

Using F-5 hook, approx 20 stitches by 18
rows over 4" square using pattern
Using G-6 hook, approx 16 stitches by 16
rows over 4" square using pattern

Dimensions

Approx 3½" x 12" at bottom, 12½" tall, 17"
across the top

To make the bag

When working with color changing,
the color not being used is worked
through the center of the stitch. For
solid row colors, the opposite color
does not need to be worked through
the center.

NOTE: Instructions are given for the
small size first, with the large size
in parentheses.

BASE (MAKE 1)
Using F-5 hook and MC, ch55(67).
Row 1: sc1 into 2nd ch from hook,
sc1 into each st to end, turn.
(54 (66)sts)
Row 2: ch1, sc1 into each st to end,
turn.
Repeat Row 2 a further 16 (28) times
or until base is the correct width.
Do not fasten off yarn.

SIDES (MAKE 1)
Change to G-6 hook and work the
sides of the bag in rounds.

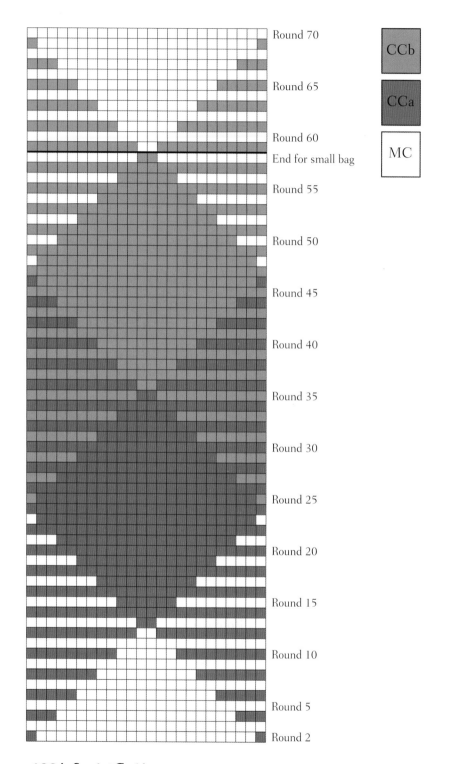

Round 70

Round 65

Round 60

End for small bag

Round 55

Round 50

Round 45

Round 40

Round 35

Round 30

Round 25

Round 20

Round 15

Round 10

Round 5

Round 2

CCb

CCa

MC

Round 1: using MC, ch1, sc1 into each st around the outer edge of the base, sl st into ch1 at beg of round. (144 (192) sts)

Do not fasten off MC; join in CCa. This color pattern is worked in a series of 24st repeats. See chart (left) for visual reference.

Round 2: using CCa, ch1, *sc1 into first st; using MC, sc1 into next 22sts; using CCa, sc1 into next st, rep from * to end, sl st into ch1 at beg of round.

Round 3: using MC, ch1, sc1 into each st to end, sl st into ch1 at beg of round.

Round 4: using CCa, ch1, *sc1 into next 3sts; using MC, sc1 into next 18sts; using CCa, sc1 into next 3sts, rep from * to end, sl st into ch1 at beg of round.

Round 5: as Round 3.

Round 6: using CCa, ch1, *sc1 into next 5sts; using MC, sc1 into next 14sts; using CCa, sc1 into next 5sts, rep from * to end, sl st into ch1 at beg of round.

Round 7: as Round 3.

Round 8: using CCa, ch1, *sc1 into next 7sts; using MC, sc1 into next 10sts; using CCa, sc1 into next 7sts, rep from * to end, sl st into ch1 at beg of round.

Round 9: as Round 3.

Round 10: using CCa, ch1, *sc1

into next 9sts; using MC, sc1 into next 6sts; using CCa, sc1 into next 9sts, rep from * to end, sl st into ch1 at beg of round.

Round 11: as Round 3.

Round 12: using CCa, ch1, *sc1 into next 11sts; using MC, sc1 into next 2sts; using CCa, sc1 into next 11sts, rep from * to end, sl st into ch1 at beg of round.

Round 13: using MC, ch1, *sc1 into next 11sts; using CCa, sc1 into next 2sts; using MC, sc1 into next 11sts, rep from * to end, sl st into ch1 at beg of round.

Round 14: using CCa, ch1, sc1 into each st to end, sl st into ch1 at beg of round.

Round 15: using MC, ch1, *sc1 into next 9sts; using CCa, sc1 into next 6sts; using MC, sc1 into next 9sts, rep from * to end, sl st into ch1 at beg of round.

Round 16: as Round 14.

Round 17: using MC, ch1, *sc1 into next 7sts; using CCa, sc1 into next 10sts; using MC, sc1 into next 7sts, rep from * to end, sl st into ch1 at beg of round.

Round 18: as Round 14.

Round 19: using MC, ch1, *sc1 into next 5sts; using CCa, sc1 into next 14sts; using MC, sc1 into next 5sts, rep from * to end, sl st into ch1 at beg of round.

Round 20: as Round 14.

Round 21: using MC, ch1, *sc1 into next 3sts; using CCa, sc1 into next 18sts; using MC, sc1 into next 3sts, rep from * to end, sl st into ch1 at beg of round.

Round 22: as Round 14.

Round 23: using MC, ch1, *sc1 into next st; using CCa, sc1 into next 22sts; using MC, sc1 into next st, rep from * to end, sl st into ch1 at beg of round.
Break off MC.

Round 24: as Round 14.
Do not break off CCa; join in CCb.

Round 25: using CCb, ch1, *sc1 into next st; using CCa, sc1 into next 22sts; using CCb, sc1 into next st, rep from * to end, sl st into ch1 at beg of round.

Round 26: as Round 14.

Round 27: using CCb, ch1, *sc1 into next 3sts; using CCa, sc1 into next 18sts; using CCb, sc1 into next 3sts, rep from * to end, sl st into ch1 at beg of round.

Round 28: as Round 14.

Round 29: using CCb, ch1, *sc1 into next 5sts; using CCa, sc1 into next 14sts; using CCb, sc1 into next 5sts, rep from * to end, sl st into ch1 at beg of round.

Round 30: as Round 14.

Round 31: using CCb, ch1, *sc1 into next 7sts; using CCa, sc1 into next 10sts; using CCb, sc1 into next 7sts, rep from * to end, sl st into ch1 at beg of round.

Round 32: as Round 14.

Round 33: using CCb, ch1, *sc1 into next 9sts; using CCa, sc1 into next 6sts; using CCb, sc1 into next 9sts, rep from * to end, sl st into ch1 at beg of round.

Round 34: as Round 14.

Round 35: using CCb, ch1, *sc1 into next 11sts; using CCa, sc1 into next 2sts; using CCb, sc1 into next 11sts, rep from * to end, sl st into ch1 at beg of round.

Round 36: using CCa, ch1, *sc1 into next 11sts; using CCb, sc1 into next 2sts; using CCa, sc1 into next 11sts, rep from * to end, sl st into ch1 at beg of round.

Round 37: using CCb, ch1, sc1 into each st to end, sl st into ch1 at beg of round.

Round 38: using CCa, ch1, *sc1 into next 9sts; using CCb, sc1 into next 6sts; using CCa, sc1 into next 9sts, rep from * to end, sl st into ch1 at beg of round.

Round 39: as Round 37.

Round 40: using CCa, ch1, *sc1 into next 7sts; using CCb, sc1 into next 10sts; using CCa, sc1 into next 7sts, rep from * to end, sl st into ch1 at beg of round.

Round 41: as Round 37.

Round 42: using CCa, ch1, *sc1 into next 5sts; using CCb, sc1 into next 14sts; using CCa, sc1 into next 5sts, rep from * to end, sl st into ch1 at beg of round.

Round 43: as Round 37.

Round 44: using CCa, ch1, *sc1 into next 3sts; using CCb, sc1 into next 18sts; using CCa, sc1 into next 3sts, rep from * to end, sl st into ch1 at beg of round.

Round 45: as Round 37.

Round 46: using CCa, ch1, *sc1 into next st; using CCb, sc1 into next 22sts; using CCa, sc1 into next st, rep from * to end, sl st into ch1 at beg of round.

Round 47: as Round 37. Fasten off CCa and rejoin MC.

Round 48: using MC, ch1, *sc1 into next st; using CCb, sc1 into next 22sts; using MC, sc1 into next st, rep from * to end, sl st into ch1 at beg of round.

Round 49: as Round 37.

Round 50: using MC, ch1, *sc1 into next 3sts; using CCb, sc1 into next 18sts; using MC, sc1 into next 3sts, rep from * to end, sl st into ch1 at beg of round.

Round 51: as Round 37.

Round 52: using MC, ch1, *sc1 into next 5sts; using CCb, sc1 into next 14sts; using MC, sc1 into next 5sts, rep from * to end, sl st into ch1 at beg of round.

Round 53: as Round 37.

Round 54: using MC, ch1, *sc1 into next 7sts; using CCb, sc1 into next 10sts; using MC, sc1 into next 7sts, rep from * to end, sl st into ch1 at beg of round.

Round 55: as Round 37.

Round 56: using MC, ch1, *sc1 into next 9sts; using CCb, sc1 into next 6sts; using MC, sc1 into next 9sts, rep from * to end, sl st into ch1 at beg of round.

Round 57: as Round 37.

Round 58: using MC, ch1, *sc1 into next 11sts; using CCb, sc1 into next 2sts; using MC, sc1 into next 11sts, rep from * to end, sl st into ch1 at beg of round.

Small bag only

Round 59: Using MC, ch1, sc1 into each st to end, sl st into ch1 at beg of round. Fasten off yarn.

Large bag only

Round 59: using CCb, ch1, *sc1 into next 11sts; using MC, sc1 into next 2sts; using CCb, sc1 into next 11sts, rep from * to end, sl st into ch1 at beg of round.

Round 60: as Round 3.

Round 61: using CCb, ch1, *sc1 into next 9sts; using MC, sc1 into next 6sts; using CCb, sc1 into next 9sts, rep from * to end, sl st into ch1 at beg of round.

Round 62: as Round 3.

Round 63: using CCb, ch1, *sc1 into next 7sts; using MC, sc1 into next 10sts; using CCb, sc1 into next 7sts, rep from * to end, sl st into ch1 at beg of round.

Round 64: as Round 3.

Round 65: using CCb, ch1, *sc1 into next 5sts; using MC, sc1 into next 14sts; using CCb, sc1 into next 5 sts, rep from * to end, sl st into ch1 at beg of round.

Round 66: as Round 3.

Round 67: using CCb, ch1, *sc1 into next 3sts; using MC, sc1 into next 18sts; using CCb, sc1 into next 3sts, rep from * to end, sl st into ch1 at beg of round.

Round 68: as Round 3.

Round 69: using CCb, ch1, *sc1 into next st; using MC, sc1 into next 22sts; using CCb, sc1 into next st, rep from * to end, sl st into ch1 at beg of round.

Round 70: as Round 3.

Fasten off yarn. Weave in loose ends.

Finishing

Using picture as guide, fold the top of the bag so the top corner of the bag is even with the center of each end of the rectangle piece at the bottom. Next, pin and then hand sew the zipper to the top of the bag, then sew the remaining open parts of the bag on each end of the zipper closed with your needle and thread.

Make loops for handle as follows. Using F-5 hook and CCb, ch9.

Row 1: sc1 into 2nd ch from hook, sc1 into each ch to end, turn. (8sts)

Row 2: ch1, sc1 into each st to end, turn.

Repeat Row 2 six more times. Fasten off yarn and weave in loose ends.

Loop square just worked through metal ring, then sew onto side of bag approx 3" from top on large bag and 1½" on small bag (see above right). Repeat this for second loop. Attach the strap. It can be latched onto each ring to make a long

cross-body bag, or folded in half and looped through one side, both latches being hooked on the opposite side to make it an over-the-shoulder bag.

Crochet TECHNIQUES

Whether you want to learn the basics, or just need to refresh your memory about one or two stitches or other techniques, you'll find all the information you need to make the projects in this book in this chapter.

Tools and Materials

Choosing the yarn for a project is great fun. However, it's important to know a little bit about the basic properties of yarns, such as their weights and fibers, before you begin. As well as yarn you will, of course, need a crochet hook to crochet with, but there are one or two other pieces of equipment you will find useful. The information below gives a brief introduction to some of the items you will need to have in your work box.

Yarns

There are three types of yarn fiber: animal, plant, and synthetic. Many yarns blend different fibers together to produce more durable yarns that can be machine washed and dried.

The most common animal fiber is sheep's wool. It is warm, insulating, absorbent, and quite elastic, making it easy to crochet with. Other commonly used animal fibers are mohair, cashmere, angora, alpaca, and silk.

Plant fibers, such as cotton, linen, hemp, soy, and bamboo, are lightweight, breathe well, and are ideal for warm-weather garments.

Synthetic (man-made) fibers include acrylic, nylon, polyester, and rayon. Yarns made from them are durable, inexpensive, and machine washable, making them perfect for items that need frequent washing.

Fibers are spun into yarns of different thicknesses referred to as "weights." The names of the different weights vary from country to country. Each one has a gauge and recommended hook size; use these as a guideline when choosing yarn, but always check your gauge (see page 115) as you want to match the gauge of the pattern you are crocheting and knowing the weight of a yarn is important should you decide to substitute one yarn for another.

You should find all the information you need to know about a yarn on the label. Most should include the knitting gauge, but not all will include the crochet gauge. If so, use the knitting gauge. Choose a hook one size larger than the recommended knitting needle size.

Always buy enough yarn in the same color and dye lot to complete a particular project.

Tools

Crochet hooks are available in many styles—from basic aluminum, wood, and plastic to ergonomic designs with molded-plastic handles. Try out a few to see which you prefer and remember that some hooks work better with different types of yarn. For example, a wooden hook will grip the yarn, making it ideal for slippery silks, while sleek aluminum hooks tend to work well with rougher woolen yarns.

The size of a modern hook will be marked on the handle—either the US letter/numbering system, or the metric size, or both. If you cannot find this, use a knitting gauge—a piece of plastic or wood with holes drilled in it. Slide the shaft of the hook into the holes until you find the perfect fit.

A small pair of scissors with sharp blades are useful for cutting and trimming yarn ends. As well as measuring your crochet, a retractable tape measure is useful when checking your gauge.

Sew in yarn ends and join sections using a blunt tapestry needle with an eye large enough to accommodate your yarn. Hold fabrics together for

sewing, and in place when blocking, with the large glass-headed, rust-free pins used by quilters. Sharper sewing needles are required when stitching your work to fabrics or cushions, as for the Sunflower Motif Pillow.

Some patterns require stitch markers to help you to keep track of the beginning of continuous rounds or pattern repeats, and for counting stitches. These can be as simple as a scrap of yarn or a safety pin, but make sure they have open ends and can be removed easily without snagging your yarn.

Designs such as the Chevron Pillow (see page 38) and the Star Backpack (see page 100) require small amounts of different colors of yarn. You will find that these are easier to work with if they are wound onto bobbins, or around small pieces of cardboard, than if you try to work with larger balls of yarn.
You can also use the bobbins to store scraps of yarn neatly.

Experiment with different colorways to create vibrant variations unique to you.

Getting Started

Holding the hook and yarn

There are two ways to hold the hook: the knife hold and the pencil hold. Use the one you find most comfortable. To create tension on the yarn so that you can form stitches evenly, hold the working yarn in your non-dominant hand.

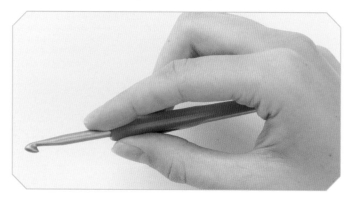

KNIFE HOLD
Hold the flat section or middle of the hook lightly between your thumb and forefinger.

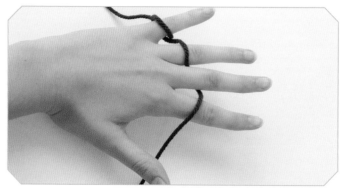

WOVEN
Weave the yarn over your index finger, under the middle finger, and over your ring finger. If this feels loose, wrap it around your pinkie.

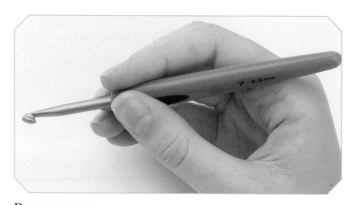

PENCIL HOLD
Use the tips of your thumb and forefinger to hold the hook lightly on the flat section or middle of the hook.

FOREFINGER
Wrap the yarn twice around your forefinger.

Gauge

For many projects in this book, checking and maintaining your gauge to ensure that your finished crochet is the correct size is not essential. However, it is necessary for some items and, for these, you should work a swatch before you start.

Each pattern will indicate the gauge. For example: 4" = 15 treble crochet (tr) and 9 rows using size H-8 hook. However, everyone's gauge is different.

To check your gauge, crochet a 6" square using the hook size, yarn, and stitch pattern (in this example, treble crochet) stated in the pattern. Place a ruler horizontally across a row of stitches in the center of the square and insert pins at the 0 and 4" marks. Then count the stitches between the pins—including any partial stitches. For this example do you have 15 stitches? If you have too many, make a second square using a hook one size larger. If you have too few, use a hook one size smaller. Keep making squares until you have the correct gauge. Check the vertical gauge in the same way, counting the number of rows between the pins—including any partial rows—and adjust the hook size as necessary.

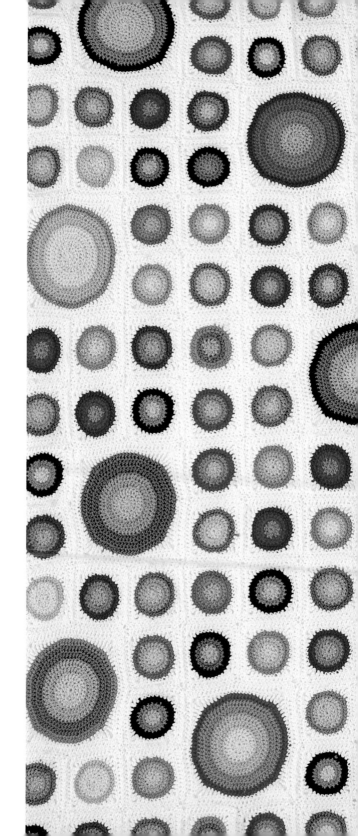

Making a slipknot

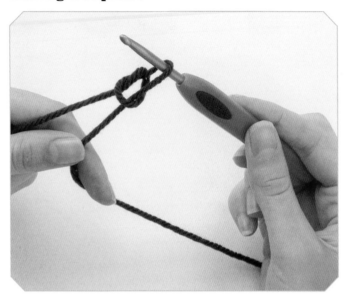

Wrap the yarn clockwise around your forefinger and cross it over the working yarn leaving a 6" tail (you will weave this in later). Insert the hook in front of the original loop but behind the tail end of the yarn. Slide the loop off your finger while pinching the X overlap you just made. Hold both yarn ends and pull them tight, but not too tight, around your hook.

Foundation chain and chain stitches

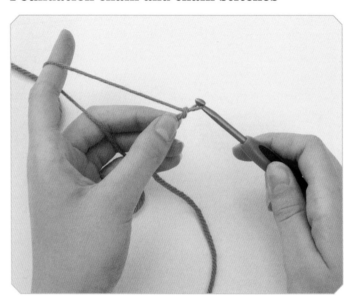

The foundation chain is a little like casting on when knitting—it's the starting point for working new stitches. As you work the chain, keep moving your fingers up the chain to hold the latest stitch. Make a slipknot on your hook and hold it with the thumb and middle finger of your yarn hand. Bring the working yarn from behind and over the hook (this is referred to as a "yarn over the hook"). Use the hook to pull the yarn through the loop on your hook. You have made one chain stitch. Repeat to make the required number of chains, but remember that the loop on your hook never counts as a chain stitch.

Working into the chain

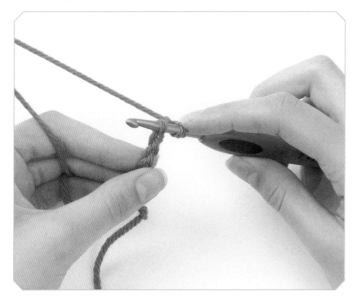

The first row of crochet stitches is worked into the chain. From the front each chain forms a V shape; from the back each one has a ridge that forms a spine. There are three ways to do this, each one giving a different result. Working through the top loop of the chain is the simplest method but may leave gaps between the stitches. Working through the back ridge only will give the first row the same look as the last, making it ideal if you are not giving your finished project a border or edging. Alternatively you can work through the top loop and back ridge at the same time.

Turning chains

Turning chains are essential to bring the first stitch of a row or round up to the proper height. This is why a pattern will tell you to skip chains before you work your first stitch into the foundation chain. A slip stitch does not require a turning chain. Single crochet has one chain but this is not counted as a stitch. Half double crochet has two turning chains; these sometimes count as a stitch. Double crochet requires three turning chains and these are counted as a stitch. Four chains are used with treble crochet and these also count as a stitch.

Stitches

Single crochet (sc)

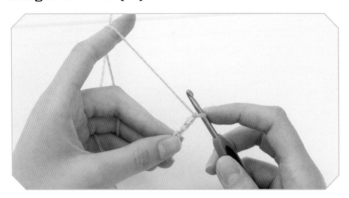

1 Insert the hook into the second chain from the hook.

3 Yarn over the hook and pull it through both loops on the hook to complete the stitch. Insert the hook into the next chain and repeat Steps 2 and 3. Repeat this sequence into each chain.

2 Yarn over the hook and pull up a loop to make two loops on the hook.

4 To work the next row, make one chain and turn the work. Insert the hook into the first stitch under the top two loops and complete Steps 2 and 3. Continue across the row. Do not work a stitch into the turning chain of the previous row.

Half double crochet (hdc)

1 Yarn over the hook and insert the hook into the third chain from the hook.

2 Yarn over the hook and pull up a loop to make three loops on the hook.

3 Yarn over the hook and draw through all three loops on the hook to complete the stitch. Yarn over the hook, insert the hook into the next chain, and complete Steps 2 and 3. Repeat into each chain across.

4 To work the next row, make two chains and turn the work. Insert the hook into the second stitch (skipping the first stitch because the two turning chains count as a stitch).

5 Work under the top two loops and complete Steps 2 and 3. Continue working stitches into each stitch across the row. Make the last stitch into the top chain of the previous row's turning chain.

Counting the two turning chains as a stitch can leave gaps in the row edges. As a result, some patterns do not count them as a stitch. If this is the case, work the first stitch of the row into the first stitch, and do not work a stitch into the turning chain at the end of the row. Follow the pattern instructions closely and make sure the stitch count for each row or round matches the stitch count given in the pattern.

Double crochet (dc)

1 Yarn over the hook and insert the hook into the fourth chain from the hook.

3 Yarn over the hook and draw through two loops. There will be two loops on the hook.

5 To work the next row, make three chains and turn the work. Insert the hook into the second stitch (skipping the first stitch because the three turning chains count as a stitch). Work under the top two loops and complete Steps 2 to 4.

2 Yarn over the hook and pull up a loop. There will be three loops on the hook.

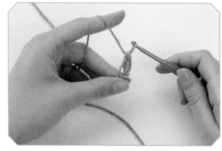

4 Yarn over the hook and draw through two loops to complete the stitch. Yarn over the hook, insert the hook into the next chain, and complete Steps 2 to 4. Repeat into each chain across.

6 Continue working stitches into each stitch across the row. The last stitch will be made into the top chain of the previous row's turning chain.

Treble crochet (tr)

1 Yarn over the hook twice and insert the hook into the fifth chain from the hook.

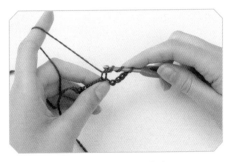

3 Yarn over the hook and draw through two loops. There will be three loops on the hook.

5 Yarn over the hook and draw through two loops to complete the stitch. Yarn over the hook twice and insert the hook into the next chain and complete Steps 2 to 5. Repeat into each chain across.

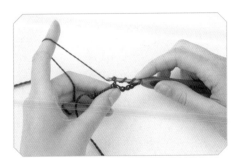

2 Yarn over the hook and pull up a loop. There will be four loops on the hook.

4 Yarn over the hook and draw through two loops. There will be two loops on the hook.

6 To work the next row, make four chains and turn the work. Insert the hook into the second stitch (skipping the first stitch because the four turning chains count as a stitch). Work under the top two loops and complete Steps 2 to 5. Continue across the row. Make the last stitch into the top chain of the previous row's turning chain.

Slip stitch (sl st)

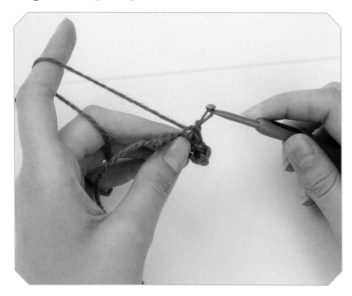

This stitch is rarely used to create crochet fabrics on its own. Instead it is used to join crochet fabrics together, work across a set of stitches without adding height, join rounds, or reinforce an edge.

To create a slip stitch in a foundation chain, insert the hook into the second chain from the hook. Yarn over the hook and draw it through the loop on the hook. To work the next row, turn the work without adding a turning chain and slip stitch into the first stitch of the row.

Working double treble (dtr) and triple treble (trtr) crochet

Some patterns use the longer double treble, and even longer triple treble. These are worked in a similar manner to the treble crochet on the page 121. For the double treble, yarn over the hook three times and draw through two loops each time until stitch is complete. For the triple treble, yarn over the hook four times and draw through two loops each time until stitch is complete.

Working into the front and back of stitches

Working around the post of a stitch creates decorative ridges and texture in the crocheted fabric. They are sometimes called relief or raised stitches.

Front post double crochet (FPdc)

1 Wrap the yarn around the hook and insert the hook from the front to the back of the fabric, taking it around the back of the post of the stitch. Bring it out at the front of the fabric. Yarn over the hook again and pull up a loop on the right side of the fabric (three loops on hook).

2 Yarn over the hook and draw it through the first two loops on the hook. Yarn over the hook again and draw it through the remaining two loops (one front post double crochet made).

Back post double crochet (BPdc)
1 Wrap the yarn around the hook and insert the hook from the back to the front, taking it around the front of the post of the stitch, and bring it out at the back of the crochet. Yarn over the hook again and pull up a loop on the wrong side of the fabric (three loops on hook).

3 Yarn over the hook again and draw it through the remaining two loops (one back post double crochet made).

2 Yarn over the hook and draw it through the first two loops on the hook.

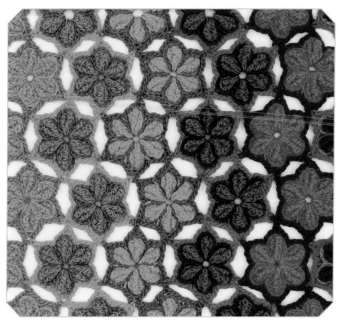

Increasing and Decreasing Stitches

Basic shaping is a simple matter of increasing and decreasing the number of stitches. These techniques are necessary for many crochet projects. Decrease stitches are worked over more than one stitch, and combine several stitches in each stitch. The technique for a one-stitch decrease is shown below for each of the four basic crochet stitches.

To increase one or more stitches within a row or round

Work more than one stitch into a stitch of the previous row or round. Here the increase is shown in double crochet, but the method is the same for all the other crochet stitches.

To increase several stitches at the beginning of a row

Work the number of turning chains required for the stitch plus an extra chain for each additional stitch you want to add. Skip the required number of turning chains and then work a stitch into the remaining chains to complete the increase.

To increase several stitches at the end of a row

1 Work extended stitches. For extended double crochet, insert the hook into the same stitch as the last double crochet of the row. *Pull up a loop, yarn over the hook, and draw through one loop only. Mark the chain stitch you have made.

2 Yarn over the hook and draw through the two loops on your hook to complete the stitch. Insert your hook into the marked chain and repeat from * to create the next stitch.

Single crochet decrease (sc2tog)

1 Insert the hook into the first stitch and pull up a loop. Insert the hook into the next stitch and pull up a loop. There will be three loops on the hook.

2 Yarn over the hook and draw through all three loops.

Half double crochet decrease (hdc2tog)

1 Yarn over the hook, insert the hook into the first stitch, and pull up a loop. Yarn over the hook, insert the hook into the next stitch, and pull up a loop. There will be five loops on the hook. For a less bulky half treble crochet decrease, omit this yarn over the hook.

2 Yarn over the hook and draw through all five loops.

Double crochet decrease (dc2tog)

1 Yarn over the hook, insert the hook into the first stitch, and pull up a loop. Yarn over the hook and draw through two loops on the hook. Yarn over the hook, insert the hook into the next stitch, and pull up a loop. Yarn over the hook and draw through two loops. There will be three loops on the hook.

2 Yarn over the hook and draw through all three loops to complete the decrease.

Treble crochet decrease (tr2tog)

1 This decrease is worked in a similar way to the double crochet decrease. Work a treble crochet into the first stitch until there are two loops on the hook, omitting the last step.

3 Yarn over the hook and draw through all three loops to complete the decrease.

2 Yarn over the hook twice, insert the hook into the next stitch, and work a treble crochet until three loops remain on the hook.

Working in the Round

Working crochet in the round is essential for motifs such as granny squares (see page 132). There are three methods of beginning a round and most patterns will have instructions for which method to use, but feel free to use a different method if none is suggested by the pattern.

Making a joined round of chains

This method is ideal if the first round has a large number of stitches, as it enables the stitches of the first round to lie flat without bunching or overlapping, but it will leave a hole in the center of the fabric. You can also add additional chains to accommodate more stitches in the beginning round.

Make a short chain. Join the chain into a ring by making a slip stitch into the first chain. Work a turning chain (see page 117) to bring the round up to the height of the stitches, then work the first round of stitches into the ring. Work a slip stitch into the top chain of the turning chain to join the first round together.

Creating a round of stitches by working into one chain

This method is easy to work but it is not a good choice if there are a large number of stitches in the first round as it will be overcrowded and the stitches will not lie flat. However it will give you a tight center without a hole.

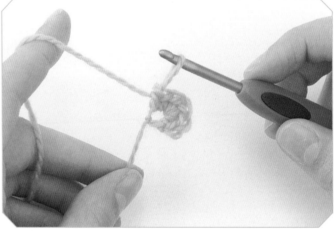

For example, make two chains and work six double crochet stitches into the second chain from the hook. Work under the top loop only of the chain stitch as this will allow you to expand and tighten the chain as needed.

Magic loop

The magic loop or ring can be used to create a round with a tight center and a lot of stitches. However, it is not suitable for slippery yarns because the yarn end may work loose.

1 Wind the working yarn around your forefinger and cross it over the tail yarn, leaving a 6" tail.

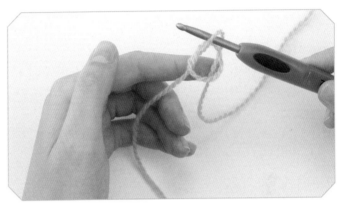

3 Insert the hook through the front of the loop, pull through a loop of the working yarn and hold it on the hook with your forefinger.

2 Slide the loop off your finger while pinching the X overlap you have made.

4 Yarn over the hook and work a chain stitch to secure. Crochet over both the magic loop and yarn tail as you complete the first round. Pull the yarn tail to tighten.

Working flat rounds

To keep crocheted fabric flat while working in rounds, work increase stitches evenly on each round.

1 Work a round of stitches and slip stitch into the first stitch to join it. Make a turning chain to bring the round to the correct height, but do not turn the work (unless instructed to do so in the pattern). The turning chain will count as a stitch. Work two stitches into each stitch of the previous round for Round 2.

2 For subsequent rounds, increase the stitch count by the same number of stitches as Round 1.

Working tubular rounds

1 Work a length of chain stitches equal to the diameter of the finished tube. Slip stitch into the first chain to join the round. Work a turning chain to bring the round up to height. Work one stitch into each chain, being careful not to twist the chain, and join the round at the end. To create a straight seam, turn the work at the end of each round; otherwise, there will be a slanted seam.

2 Work the following rounds evenly (one stitch in each stitch). To create a tube with a closed end, work flat rounds to the diameter required for the tube to make the closed end, then work evenly until the tube is the desired height.

Joining in New Colors

Whether you need to join in a new color of yarn at the beginning or in the middle of a row, the method is the same. Use the same technique for joining in a new ball of the same yarn color, but note that this is best done at the beginning of a row.

1 Work the last stitch but stop at the last step before drawing through the final yarn over the hook. There will be two loops on the hook.

2 Drop the old color behind the work and draw the new color through to complete the stitch. Continue working with the color as usual.

Granny Squares and Other Motifs

Granny squares are traditional crochet motifs usually created by working a series of rounds, increasing the number of stitches each time. The most common form uses double crochet, but there are may other variations you can try. These motifs are quick and easy to make whether you're at home or out and about. They are also a great way to use up scraps of yarn and many crocheters find them more satisfying to work than row after row of stitches. Traditionally, each round of a motif is worked in a different color, but you can also make single-color motifs. They are also a great way to explore different color combinations.

Joining motifs

Motifs can be joined together with sewn or crocheted seams and the seams can become part of the design. Align the stitches carefully before you start to join them. You may find it easiest to pin them together. Join irregular-shaped motifs using the "join as you go" method described here by incorporating the joins into the last round of the second and each subsequent motif.

2 Continue to work the second motif in the established pattern up to the next chain 2 space, but do not chain 2. Repeat Steps 1 and 2 for the next join.

1 For example, chain 1, then insert the hook from front to back into any chain 2 space of the first motif. Work a slip stitch and chain 1 to complete the join.

3 Complete the final round of the second motif as established in the pattern. Add more motifs until you have the desired length.

Finishing your Work

Finishing

When you have worked your last stitch, you need to cut the yarn and fasten off. Do not cut the yarn too close to the stitches—about 6" will leave you enough to weave into the stitches to secure it.

1 Cut the yarn, wrap it around the hook, and pull it through the last stitch on the hook.

2 Pull the yarn tail tight to fasten off, then weave in.

Weaving in ends

The final instructions of any crochet pattern usually include the words "weave in the loose ends." On a project with many colors this may seem time-confusing, but it is essential for a neat, professional finish.

The best tool for the job is a tapestry needle with a large eye and blunt tip. Thread the yarn tail onto it and, working on the wrong side of the fabric, pull the yarn through at least 2" of stitches, making sure the needle goes through the loops of the stitches and not the yarn itself. Then weave it back in the opposite direction for 1" to prevent the end from working loose.

Blocking

Blocking a piece of crochet before using it or sewing it to other pieces to create an item of clothing creates a neat finish and makes sewing seams much easier. It means that the final pieces will be the correct size and the stitches will be shown to the best advantage.

There are two methods you can use: cold water and steam. Cold water blocking is used for synthetic man-made yarns, such as acrylic and nylon yarns that would be damaged by the heat of steam blocking. Pin the crochet to the correct size on a folded towel or ironing board with the right side facing up. Spray with cold water to dampen it, but do not over-saturate it, and allow it to dry completely before removing the pins.

Steam blocking is only suitable for natural fibers, such as wool and cotton. Place the iron over the piece and allow the steam to set the stitches. Never press the iron directly onto the piece being blocked, because this will flatten and distort the stitches.

Seams and Joining

Take time when sewing your crochet sections together so that the finished item is neat and reflects the time you have taken to create it. There are several ways to join seams and you can use more than one method in a project if you wish. If you want a hidden seam, then mattress stitch is a good choice. Use the same yarn you used to crochet the item. If you want the seam to become part of the finished design, choose a slip stitch or a single crochet seam. You could also use a contrasting color yarn to add decorative detail.

Mattress stitch

This seam has no bulk and it is used frequently in garment construction. Place the crocheted pieces on a flat surface with the right sides facing up, making sure the stitches are aligned. Insert the needle through the post of the bottom right stitch, cross over to the corresponding left stitch, and at the same time draw the yarn through the post of the stitch. Continue working backward and forward through the posts of the stitches. Gently tighten the seam while you work, but don't make it too tight.

Top seams

Top seams can be joined with single crochet (see page 118) or slip stitches (see page 122). Slip stitch creates a flat seam but it will not have as much stretch as a single crochet seam.

SLIP STITCH SEAM

Hold the two pieces of crochet to be joined with right sides facing each other. Insert the hook through the first stitch of both pieces, and the pull yarn through to make a slip stitch. Insert the hook through the next stitch of both pieces, yarn over the hook, and pull the yarn through both the stitches and the loop on the hook. Continue to the end of the seam.

SINGLE CROCHET SEAM

Work in the same way as slip stitch, using single crochet.

Whipstitch

This stitch is quick to work and is especially useful on straight-edged fabrics. It's a good choice for joining motifs together. With the right sides of the fabric pieces held together, insert the needle from the front to the back of a stitch and through the corresponding stitch on the other piece. Bring the needle to the front again and repeat until the seam is finished

Backstitch

This sturdy seam has some bulk to it, so test it first to see if it's an appropriate seam for your crocheted fabric. With the right sides of the fabric pieces held together and working about one stitch space away from the edge of the fabric, insert the needle from the back to the front through both thicknesses. Insert the needle from the front to the back of the fabric and then bring it up through to the front again one stitch beyond the working yarn. For the next stitch, insert the needle from the front to the back in the same place as the last stitch ended and again bring the needle to the front one stitch beyond the working yarn. Repeat until the seam is finished.

Reading Patterns

Crochet patterns are a step-by-step guide to creating a finished item. They usually include information about the materials, gauge, measurements, or finished size, as well as step-by-step instructions and abbreviations. Some also include color charts that offer a visual representation of the pattern.

Punctuation

Patterns are a concise and easy-to-read set of instructions that use abbreviations and punctuation to help avoid needless repetition. Once you understand them you will find following the pattern becomes automatic.

( ) ROUND BRACKETS give additional information about a pattern. For example (dc12) listed at the end of a row says that you should have 12 double crochet stitches when the row has been completed.

CH 3 (COUNTS AS FIRST DC) explains that the three turning chains count as a double crochet stitch and the stitch is included in the instructions for the stitch count at the end of the row or round.

[ ] SQUARE BRACKETS designate a set of stitch instructions, such as [dc1, ch3, dc1]. This means that you will double crochet, chain 3, double crochet all in the same stitch. It may also contain a stitch repeat—[dc1, ch3, dc1] twice. For this, you will double crochet, chain 3, double crochet all in the same stitch twice.

* AN ASTERISK indicates stitch instructions and pattern repeats on a row or round. *Dc1, ch1, skip next st. Rep from * 4 more times to last st, dc1. This instruction tells you to double crochet, chain 1, skip the next stitch. Repeat four more times, and then double crochet into the last stitch.

Color charts

Color charts may be a complete chart or a section that represents color placement. Each stitch is represented by a square, so written instructions are not necessary (although some patterns may give both written and charted instructions). A legend to the symbols will be given with the chart.

The crochet patterns in this book have been given a skill level to help you to determine the complexity of the designs. See page 139 for more information.

See page 139 for more information.

Skill Level key

✿✿✿✿	EXPERIENCED
✿✿✿	INTERMEDIATE
✿✿	EASY
✿	BEGINNER

Abbreviations

The patterns in this book feature a number of standard abbreviations, which are explained below. These abbreviations are logical and easy to understand. Any abbreviations that are exclusive to one pattern are listed and explained with that pattern.

beg	beginning	**MC**	main color
blo	back loop only	**meas**	measures
BP	back post	**rem**	remaining
CC	contrasting color	**rep**	repeat
ch	chain	**RS**	right side
cl	cluster	**sc**	single crochet
dc	double crochet	**sl st**	slip stitch
dc2tog	double crochet next 2 sts together	**sp(s)**	space(s)
dc3tog	double crochet next 3 sts together	**st(s)**	stitches
dtr	double treble	**tch**	turning chain
flo	front loop only	**tr**	treble
foll	following	**tr2tog**	treble next 2 sts together
FPdc	front post double crochet	**tr3tog**	treble next 3 sts together
FPtr	front post treble crochet	**trtr**	triple treble
gr	group	**WS**	wrong side
hdc	half double crochet	**yo**	yarn over hook
hdc2tog	half double crochet next 2 sts together		

Useful Information

YARN WEIGHTS

Yarn-Weight Symbol and Category Name	**1** Super Fine	**2** Fine	**3** Light	**4** Medium	**5** Bulky	**6** Super Bulky
Types of Yarn in Category	Sock, Fingering, Baby	Sport, Baby	DK, Light Worsted	Worsted, Afghan, Aran	Chunky, Craft, Rug	Bulky, Roving
Crochet Gauge Ranges* in Single Crochet to 4"	21 to 32sts	16 to 20sts	12 to 17sts	11 to 14sts	8 to 11sts	5 to 9sts
Recommended Hook in Metric Size Range	2.25 to 3.5 mm	3.5 to 4.5 mm	4.5 to 5.5 mm	5.5 to 6.5 mm	6.5 to 9 mm	9 mm and larger
Recommended Hook in US Size Range	B-1 to E-4	E-4 to 7	7 to I-9	I-9 to K-10½	K-10½ to M-13	M-13 and larger

These are guidelines only. The above reflect the most commonly used gauges and needle or hook sizes for specific yarn categories.

Crochet Hook Sizes

Millimeter	US Size*
2.25 mm	B-1
2.75 mm	C-2
3.25 mm	D-3
3.5 mm	E-4
3.75 mm	F-5
4 mm	G-6
4.5 mm	7
5 mm	H-8
5.5 mm	I-9
6 mm	J-10
6.5 mm	K-10½
8 mm	L-11
9 mm	M/N-13
10 mm	N/P-15

Letter or number may vary. Rely on the millimeter sizing.

Steel Hook Sizes

Millimeter	US Size*
2.75 mm	1
2.25 mm	2
1.65 mm	7

Metric Conversions

Yards x .91 = meters
Meters x 1.09 = yards
Ounces x 28.35 = grams
Grams x .035 = ounces

Skill Levels

Each project has been given a skill-level rating.

❋ Beginner: Projects for first-time crocheters using basic stitches; minimal shaping.

❋❋ Easy: Projects using yarn with basic stitches, repetitive stitch patterns, simple color changes, and simple shaping and finishing.

❋❋❋ Intermediate: Projects using a variety of techniques, such as basic lace patterns or color patterns; midlevel shaping and finishing.

❋❋❋❋ Experienced: Projects with intricate stitch patterns, techniques, and dimension, such as nonrepeating patterns, multicolor techniques, fine threads, small hooks, detailed shaping, and refined finishing.

Yarns Used in the Projects

Vintage Fan Ripple Blanket
Scheepjeswol Softfun; 60% cotton 40% acrylic, 1.76 oz/50 g, 153 yds/140 m).
2 balls in each color: CCa sh2531 Olive, CCb 2 sh2514 Rose, CCc sh2466 Skin, CCd sh2449 Coral, CCe sh2519 Violet, CCf sh2496 Soft Yellow, CCg sh2432 Light Blue.

Annie Blanket
Drops Muskat DK; 100% cotton, 1.76 oz/ 50 g, 109 yds/100 m.
MC 5 balls in sh18 White scraps in the following colors for the stripes: Denim Blue, Light Olive, Light Pink, Vanilla Yellow, Light Blue Purple, Bordeaux, Ice Blue, Rust, Silver Green, Wine, Dark Orange, Peach.

Daisy Baby Blanket
Rosarios4 Regata; 100% cotton 3.5 oz/100 g, 299 yds/273 m.
MC 2 balls in sh01 Cream, 1 ball in each contrasting color: CCa sh25 Orange, CCb sh29 Light Orange, CCc sh33 Yellow, CCd sh61 Light Pink, CCe sh50 Dark Pink, CCf sh99 Purple, CCg sh03 Beige, CCh sh102 Green.

Color Wheel Hexagon Blanket
Drops Safran; 100% cotton, 1.76 oz/50 g, 175 yds./160 m.
MC 16 balls in 17 White, approx 1 oz/25 g each of 24 additional colors.

Happy Colors Blanket
Drops Safran; 100% cotton, 1.76 oz/50 g, 175 yds/160 m.
MC 15 x balls in sh 17 White, 29 oz/800 g in total of other colors.

Flower Power Runner
Drops Paris; 100% cotton yarn, 1.76 oz/50 g, 83 yds/75 m.
MC 1 ball in sh35 Vanilla, scraps of 15 contrast colors.

Star Fruit Rug
Stitch Nation Full O' Sheep; 100% Peruvian Wool, 4 oz/100 g, 155 yds/142 m.
1 skein in each color: CCa Poppy, CCb Clementine, CCc Honeycomb, CCd Meadow, CCe Thyme, CCf Aquamarine, CCg Mediterranean, CCh Peony, CCi Plummy.

Large Granny-Square Pillow
Phildar Phil Coton 3; 100% cotton, 1.76 oz/50 g, 132 yds/121 m.
1 ball each in 8 contrast colors.

Sunflower Motif Pillow
King Cole Bamboo Cotton; 50% cotton 50% bamboo, 3.5 oz/100 g, 250 yds/230 m.
MC 1 ball in sh 538 Cream, scraps in 4 colors.

Chevron Pillow
Drops Paris; 100% cotton 1.76 oz/50 g, 83 yds/75 m.
MC 5 balls in sh17 Off White, 1 ball in each contrasting color: sh41 Mustard, sh35 Vanilla, sh46 Rust, sh32 Light Blue Purple, sh102 Spray Blue, sh26 Dark Beige, sh59 Light Old Pink, sh25 Moss Green.

Round Floor Pillow
Phildar Phil Coton 3; 100% cotton, 1.76 oz/50 g, 132 yds/121 m.
1 ball each in 7 colors.

Spoke Mandala
Drops Paris; 100% cotton, 1.76 oz/50 g, 83 yds/75 m.
Scraps in 8 colors.

Picot-Edge Mandala
Drops Paris; 100% cotton, 1.76 oz/50 g, 83 yds/75 m.
Scraps in 12 colors.

Mandala Stool Cover
Red Heart Stitch Nation Washable Ewe; 100% superwash wool, 3.5 oz/100 g, 183 yds/167 m.
1 skein in each color: CCa sh3652 Clover, CCb sh3711 Icing, CCc sh3525 Dragonfly, CCd sh3501 Robin's Egg, CCe sh3215 Duckling, CCf sh3706 Zinnia, CCg sh3582 Lilac.
Red Heart Stitch Nation Bamboo Ewe; 55% viscose bamboo, 45% wool, 3½ oz/100 g, 177 yds/162 m.
CCh 1 skein in sh 5625 Sprout.
Paton's Classic Wool; 100% wool, 3½ oz/ 100 g, 210 yds/192 m.
1 skein in each color: CCi sh77404 Orchid, CCj sh77253 Burnt Orange, CCk sh77132 Royal Blue.
Lion Brand Wool Ease; 80% acrylic, 20% wool, 3 oz/85 g, 197 yds/180 m.
CCl 1 skein in sh191 Violet.
Lion Brand Pound of Love; 100% acrylic, 16 oz/448 g, 1,020 yds/932 m.
CCm 1 skein in Antique White.

Heart and Flower Motifs
Annell Cotton 8; 100% cotton, 1.76 oz/50 g, 186 yds/170 m.
Scraps in several colors.

Crocheted Christmas Baubles

Rico Essentials Cotton; 100% cotton, 1.76 oz/50 g, 142 yds/130 m.
Scraps in 4 colors.

Butterfly Pot Holders

Scheepjeswol Softfun; 60% cotton 40% acrylic, 1.76 oz/50 g, 153 yds/140 m.
Scraps in 7 colors.

Lace Crochet Coasters

Drops Paris; 100% cotton, 1.76 oz/50 g, 83 yds/75 m.
1 ball each in 6 graduated colors.
Annell Cotton 8; 100% cotton, 1.76 oz/50 g, 186 yds/170 m.
1 ball for edging.

Breakfast Cozy Set

Rico Creative Cotton; 100% cotton, 1.76 oz/50 g, 93 yds/85 m.
Scraps in 5 colors.

Drops of Color Headband

Drops Paris; 100% cotton, 1.76 oz/50 g, 83 yds/75 m.
Scraps in sh35 Vanilla, sh41 Mustard, sh14 Strong Yellow, sh38 Raspberry, sh37 Rusty Red, sh42 Army, sh44 Brown.

Floral Bobby Pins

Annell Cotton 8; 100% cotton, 1.76 oz/50 g, 185 yds/170 m.
A selection of colors.

Rainbow Wrist Cuffs

Debbie Bliss Baby Cashmerino; 55% wool 33% acrylic 12% cashmere, 1.76 oz/50 g, 136 yds/125 m.
1 ball in each color: MC sh026 Duck Egg, CCa sh034 Red, CCb sh006 Candy Pink, CCc sh204 Baby Blue, CCd sh071 Royal, CCe sh006 Amber, CCf sh608 Pale Lilac, CCg sh059 Mallard, CCh sh018 Citrus.

Slouch Hat

TreLiz chunky; 100% baby alpaca yarn, 3½ oz/100 g, 109 yds/100 m.
1 skein in Orange Pink Orchid.

Dancing Hearts Wrap

Anne Geddes Baby acrylic sportweight yarn by Red Heart Yarns; 3.5 oz/100 g, 340 yds/311 m.
1 ball in each color: MC sh100 Lilly, CCa sh623 Spearmint, CCb sh691 Grass, CCc sh702 Rosie, CCd sh763 Taffy.

Wildflowers Scarf

Katia Merino; 100% wool, 1.76 oz/50 g, 111 yds/102 m or Rico Design Essentials Cotton DK; 1.76 oz/50 g, 142 yds/130 m.
6 oz (175 g) in total.

Ombré String Cowl

Lion Brand Vanna's Choice; 100% acrylic, 3.5 oz/100 g, 170 yds/156 m.
Scraps in MC sh141 Wild Berry, CCa sh144 Magenta, CCb sh143 Antique Rose, CCc sh142 Rose, CCd sh138 Pink Poodle (approx 150 yds/137 m in total).

Blossom Necklace

Debbie Bliss Rialto 4 ply; 100% extra fine merino wool, 1.76 oz/50 g, 197 yds/180 m or DMC Natura Just Cotton; 100% cotton, 1.76 oz/50 g, 170 yds/155 m.
Scraps in several colors.

Granny-Square Clutch Purse

Phildar Phil coton 3; 100% cotton, 1.76 oz/50 g, 132 yds/121 m.
MC 1 ball in 010 Blanc, scraps in 8 colors.

Cell Phone and Tablet Covers

Sirdar Snuggly DK; 45% acrylic, 55% nylon, 1.76 oz/50 g, 179 yds/165 m.
1 ball in each color: CCa sh0252 Lemon, CCb sh0403 Wobble, CCc sh0420 Lolly, CCd sh0242 Flamenco, CCf sh0439 Little Bud, CCd sh0440 Blue Bud, CCg sh0441 Little Bow.

Star Backpack

Phildar Cotton Phil 3; 100% cotton, 1.76 oz/50 g, 132 yds./121 m) or Schachemayr Catania; 100% cotton 1.76 oz/50 g, 137 yds/125 m.
1 ball each in 14 contrast colors.

The Weekender Bag

Lion Brand Vanna's Choice worsted weight yarn; 100% acrylic, 3.5 oz/100 g, 170 yds/156 m.
Small Bag MC 2 balls in sh 305 Pearl Mist, 1 ball in each contrasting color: CC1 130 Honey, CC2 158 Mustard. Large Bag MC 2 balls in sh 305 Pearl Mist, 1 ball in each contrasting color: CC1 sh135 Rust, CC2 sh134 Terra Cotta.

Index

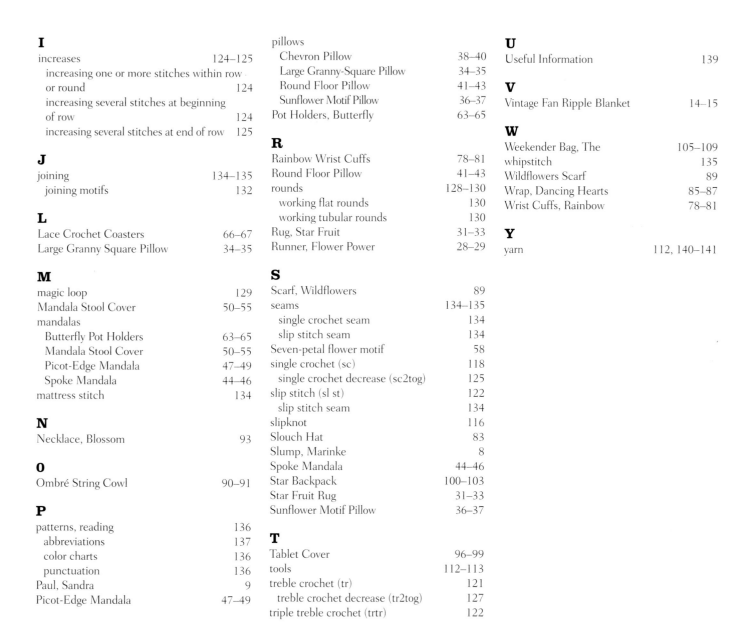

Acknowledgments

· ·

The publishers would like to thank Marinke Slump for providing the inspiration for this book, and all those who contributed their beautiful designs: Amy Astle, Annemarie Benthem, Ruth Bramham, Ali Campbell, Susan Carlson, Sara Dudek, Carmen Heffernan, Dorien Hollewijn, and Sandra Paul.